The media's watching Vault!
Here's a sampling of our coverage.

"With reviews and profiles of firms that one associate calls 'spot on', [Vault's] guide has become a key reference for those who want to know what it takes to get hired by a law firm and what to expect once they get there."

– *New York Law Journal*

"The best place on the web to prepare for a job search."

– *Fortune*

"Vault is indispensable for locating insider information."

– *Metropolitan Corporate Counsel*

"[Vault's guide] is an INVALUABLE Cliff's Notes to prepare for interviews."

– *Women's Lawyer's Journal*

"For those hoping to climb the ladder of success, [Vault's] insights are priceless."

– *Money Magazine*

"[Vault guides] make for excellent starting points for job hunters and should be purchased by academic libraries for their career sections [and] university career centers."

– *Library Journal*

VAULT

> the most trusted name in career information™

VAULT GUIDE TO THE TOP
GOVERNMENT AND NONPROFIT LEGAL EMPLOYERS

VAULT GUIDE TO THE TOP
GOVERNMENT AND NONPROFIT LEGAL EMPLOYERS

THE STAFF OF VAULT
WITH RON HOGAN

Library of Congress Cataloging-in-Publication Data

Lerner, Marcy.
  Vault guide to the top government and nonprofit legal employers /Marcy Lerner and the staff of Vault with Ron Hogan.-- 1st ed.
     p. cm.
  ISBN 1-58131-214-8
  1. Government attorneys--Vocational guidance--United States. 2. Lawyers--Vocational guidance--United States. 3. Administrative agencies--United States--Directories. 4. Nonprofit organizations--United States--Directories. 5. Corporate legal departments--United States--Directories. I. Title: Guide to the top government and nonprofit legal employers. II. Title: Top government and nonprofit legal employers. III. Hogan, Ron. IV. Vault (Firm) V. Title.
  KF299.G6L47 2003
  331.7'6134973--dc21

                                                                              2003008349

Printed in the United States of America

ACKNOWLEDGEMENTS

Matt Doull, Ahmad Al-Khaled, Lee Black, Eric Ober, Hollinger Ventures, Tekbanc, New York City Investment Fund, Globix, Hoover's, Glenn Fischer, Mark Hernandez, Ravi Mhatre, Carter Weiss, Ken Cron, Ed Somekh, Isidore Mayrock, Zahi Khouri, Sana Sabbagh, and other Vault investors, as well as our family and friends.

Psst...
Need a Change in Venue?

Use the Internet's most targeted

job search tools for law

professionals.

Vault Law Job Board

The most comprehensive and convenient job board for law professionals. Target your search by area of law, function, and experience level, and find the job openings that you want. No surfing required.

VaultMatch Resume Database

Vault takes match-making to the next level: post your resume and customize your search by area of law, experience and more. We'll match job listings with your interests and criteria and e-mail them directly to your inbox.

Table of Contents

INTRODUCTION   1

A Guide to this Guide 2

THE SCOOP   5

Trends in the Legal Industry 5

Guide to Government Recruiting 6

Guide to Nonprofit Recruiting 9

EMPLOYER PROFILES   11

American Civil Liberties Union 12

Central Intelligence Agency (CIA) 16

Cook County State's Attorney's Office 20

DC Employment Justice Center 24

Department of Agriculture 26

Department of Commerce 30

Department of Education 34

Department of Energy 38

Department of Health and Human Services 42

Department of Housing and Urban Development (HUD) 46

Department of the Interior 50

Department of Justice (DOJ) 54

Department of Labor 60

Department of State 64

Department of the Treasury 68

Drug Enforcement Administration (DEA) 72

Environmental Protection Agency (EPA) 76

Federal Aviation Administration (FAA) 80

Federal Bureau of Investigation (FBI) 84

Federal Communications Commission (FCC) .88

Federal Election Commission (FEC) 94

Federal Emergency Management Agency (FEMA) 98

Federal Reserve Board 102

Federal Trade Commission (FTC) 106

General Accounting Office (GAO) 110

General Services Administration 114

Human Rights Watch 118

Internal Revenue Service (IRS) 124

Lawyers Committee for Human Rights 128

Lawyers' Committee for Civil Rights Under Law 132

Legal Aid Society of New York 136

Los Angeles County District Attorney 140

Mexican American Legal Defense and Educational Fund (MALDEF) . .144

Manhattan District Attorney 148

National Association for the Advancement of Colored People (NAACP)152

National Asian Pacific American Legal Consortium 156

National Association of State PIRGs 160

National Women's Law Center 164

Nuclear Regulatory Commission 168

Occupational Safety and Health Administration (OSHA) 172

Office of the Comptroller of the Currency 176

Patent and Trademark Office 180

Security and Exchange Commission (SEC) 184

Social Security Administration 188

Trial Lawyers for Public Justice 192

United States Air Force Judge Advocate General 196

United States Army Judge Advocate General .200

United States Navy Judge Advocate General .202

Vera Institute of Justice 204

Introduction

CHAPTER 1

Not everyone goes to law school because of *Ally McBeal* or *L.A. Law* – some are more influenced by *Law & Order* or *A Few Good Men*. While private corporate practice is the more financially lucrative career path, many new law students have other goals in mind when they begin their legal education. Private practice attorneys make up the fast majority of law jobs – according to the Bureau of Labor Statistics, as of 2000, there were approximately 681,000 attorneys in the U.S.; three out of every four worked in law firms or solo practices. Most of the remaining 25 percent worked in government jobs, especially at the local level. The remaining attorneys held "in-house" positions at businesses or nonprofit organizations.

Why do attorneys choose the government or nonprofit path? The money at a big law firm is certainly much better, and big-firm jobs are often more prestigious, as well. But government and nonprofit work has its advantages. For one thing, the hours are usually much better – don't expect to pull any all-nighters at a government or nonprofit employer. Government and nonprofits (especially nonprofits) are often thinly staffed, so an attorney can expect exposure to a broad range of assignments in a much shorter time frame – you won't get stuck doing document review.

But maybe the biggest allure is the chance to make a difference. While many big law firms encourage participation in pro bono projects, the amount of altruistic law practice for a big-firm lawyer pales when compared to an attorney working at a nonprofit. Similarly, an attorney working for a federal agency can influence, interpret, shape and carry out public policy or put away a dangerous criminal. Government and nonprofit work attracts lawyers who are motivated by a sense of the greater good. (This is not to say that big firm practice is anathema to the public good, but few corporate lawyers will tell you that completing an equity offering delivers the same satisfaction as getting an innocent man released from death row.)

This Guide – Vault's first devoted to government and nonprofit attorneys – includes profiles of 50 of the top employers in the government and nonprofit sector. Of course, that's only the tip of the iceberg. We've focused mainly on the federal government, as opposed to the thousands of state and local governments that employ prosecutors, defense attorneys and other lawyers. Additionally, we've got a handful of nonprofit organizations that focus exclusively on legal issues. But almost every nonprofit hires at least a few attorneys to deal with legalities. This role is similar to the chief counsel position in a corporation.

Recruiting for state and local governments varies; almost every locality has an employment office that staffs legal (and non-legal) positions. Nonprofit recruiting is a little trickier. Because many nonprofits are small and not flush with cash for recruiting, an in-house counsel position is sometimes advertised on an organization's web site and is sometimes filled only through word of mouth.

What follows is a rundown of trends affecting lawyers in government and nonprofit organization, as well as a quick guide to getting recruited by those employers. Then, finally, are our profiles, which will tell you everything a legal job seeker needs to know about the top government and nonprofit organizations. Good luck in what will surely be a rewarding legal career.

A Guide to this Guide

Each of the profiles follow the same format. Here's a guide to the entries.

Firm Facts

• **Locations:** A list of major offices.

• **Major Department/Practices:** Major divisions of government agencies, or issues given significant time and energy by a government or nonprofit employer.

• **The Stats:** Basic information about an employer, including the number of attorneys, total number of employees and leadership.

• **Uppers and Downers:** The best and worst things, respectively, about working for that particular employer, as determined by Vault's interviews and surveys with insiders at that organization. (Not all profiles include uppers and downers.)

• **Salary:** The base salary (not including bonus), as determined by Vault's research. Sources include job listings, organization web sites and government publications like the U.S. Office of Personnel Management 2002 General Schedule Salary Table.

• **Employment Contact:** The person or people the organization identifies as the preferred recipient for resumes and employment queries. We've supplied as much information as is available, including names, titles, mailing addresses, phone or fax numbers, e-mail addresses and web sites. Because each organization processes resumes differently, some may have less information than others. For example, some organizations do all hiring via the Internet; those have all job openings advertised on their web sites and have an online application process. There we'll supply only a web address. We've attempted to verify the information where possible.

The Profiles

Our profiles contain three sections: The Scoop, Getting Hired and Our Survey Says:

• **The Scoop:** The employer's history, recent important developments, major cases and other points of interest.

• **Getting Hired:** An overview of the hiring process, including qualifications needed, any on-campus recruiting procedure, the number of interviews and other tips on getting hired. This is based on Vault's research and surveys, as well as interviews with employees at the agency or organization profiled.

• **Our Survey Says:** Quotes from surveys and interviews with employees about the culture, pay, hours, training and other issues relevant to job seekers.

Because we were unable to survey attorneys at all agencies, not all profiles contain the Our Survey Says section.

Psst...
Need a Change in Venue?

Use the Internet's most targeted

job search tools for law

professionals.

Vault Law Job Board

The most comprehensive and convenient job board for law professionals. Target your search by area of law, function, and experience level, and find the job openings that you want. No surfing required.

VaultMatch Resume Database

Vault takes match-making to the next level: post your resume and customize your search by area of law, experience and more. We'll match job listings with your interests and criteria and e-mail them directly to your inbox.

The Scoop

CHAPTER 2

Trends in the Legal Industry

Wisdom of Solomon?

In January 1993, President Bill Clinton proposed a new policy regarding gays and lesbians serving in the military – the "Don't Ask, Don't Tell" rule. Previously, the military actively searched its ranks for gays and lesbians and discharged them from service. Under the "Don't Ask, Don't Tell" policy, military commanders are forbidden to inquire about or investigate the sexual orientation of their underlings, and gay personnel are not to disclose their orientation through any means. However, if it becomes known that a member of the military is a homosexual, that person is subject to discharge. The policy, though considered an improvement by some, was still controversial. Critics argued that "Don't Ask, Don't Tell" did nothing to stop discrimination against homosexuals, but merely allowed them to remain in the military as long as they kept their private life strictly under wraps – a demand not made of heterosexual service members.

The controversy spilled over into an unlikely arena – campus recruiting. Many universities and law schools have an anti-discrimination policy that prevents employers with discriminatory employment or hiring practices from using school resources to recruit. Many universities cited that policy in banning military recruiters from school campuses – including recruiting by Judge Advocate General (JAG) units, the legal corps of the branches of the armed services. Students interested in careers in the armed forces had to contact JAG and other military recruiters individually and set up interviews off campus.

A couple of mid-1990s spending bills – a Department of Defense funding bill passed in 1995 and one covering the Departments of Labor, Health and Human Services and Education passed in 1997 – contained clauses known as the Solomon Amendment. Named after Gerard B.H. Solomon, who was the U.S. Representative from New York for 20 years, the 1995 law barred universities that banned military recruiters from receiving funding of any kind (including research grants) from the Defense Department; the 1997 law extended the ban to include any kind of federal funding, except for direct student aid, which was not affected. (Rep. Solomon died in October 2001, three years after retiring from the House.)

At first, the Solomon Amendment was sparsely enforced and military recruiters met with interested students off campus. After the terrorist attacks of September 11, 2001, a renewed sense of patriotism and a new sense of military importance led to pressure on schools who had eliminated the military (both recruiters and ROTC programs) from campus to include the armed services. The pressure, which came in different degrees from government officials, alumni groups and the public at large, led to a revival of the Solomon Amendment. In late 2002, the universities – and specifically, the law schools – began to respond. High-profile law schools like Harvard, Yale, Columbia and New York University opened their doors to JAG recruiters. The law schools had billions of dollars at stake. According to the *Boston Globe*, Columbia, Harvard and Yale alone stood to lose more than $1 billion in research grants and other aid.

Though military recruiters have returned to many law school and college campuses, the debate is by no means over. At most schools, the change in policy was met with student and faculty protest, and several groups are lobbying to reverse the Solomon Amendment. Meanwhile, administrators have pledged to continue allowing JAG and military recruiters on campus, despite widespread criticism of the "Don't Ask, Don't Tell" policy.

Guide to Government Recruiting

Uncle Sam wants lawyers

Forget about big-firm recruiting machines – the federal government is a big-time legal recruiter. According to the U.S. Census Bureau, as of March 2001, the federal government employed close to 58,000 people in "judicial and legal" positions. The statistics pertain only to civilian personnel and don't get more specific. Additionally, lawyers working in other positions (e.g., law enforcement) aren't included, so the actual number of JDs (or LLMs, etc.) may be higher.

There are some basic conditions anyone considering a legal career within the federal government must meet. Since 1976 nearly every civil service job has required American citizenship or residency in American Samoa. Male job applicants also need to be registered with the Selective Service, the government's draft registry. Of course, a law degree is required, but as with most law firms, many government agencies have an honors program which allows law graduates to start working as a law clerk for up to a year before passing the bar exam.

If you were in the military before earning your law degree, you may be eligible for veterans' preference when considered for government jobs. The preference generally only applies to those members of the armed forces who actually saw combat action, so you'll need to have (1) participated in an officially recognized military campaign or expedition, and (2) received a campaign badge.

The government is a drug-free workplace, and the application process for most positions will include a screening test. Jobs at law enforcement or intelligence gathering agencies require a more extensive background check that can take months to complete. In addition to speaking with friends and family, government investigators interview professors and classmates, former bosses and co-workers, even old landlords and ex-spouses. They also do a thorough reading of tax records and check for any credit problems or arrests, building up a detailed history that can extend as far as a decade into the past. (Although standards vary from agency to agency, previous drug use won't necessarily be a disqualifying factor, depending on its extent and how long ago it occurred. For example, some agencies will tolerate occasional marijuana use provided it hasn't occurred within the last five years.)

Down with OPM

Although many of the federal agencies listed in this guide will have job openings posted on their web sites, most applications or applicants go through the Office of Personnel Management (OPM), the government's own HR department, usually early in the process. The OPM has created a standardized "optional application for federal employment," also known as the OF-612, which identifies the minimum information you'll need to provide about work experience, education and other job-related qualifications; although it is not required, it is a common and useful substitute for a resumé. (The file is available for download in PDF or Word version at http://www.opm.gov/forms/html/of.asp.) Once this form is submitted, along with whatever additional materials are required in the vacancy announcement, you will be contacted directly by the agency to which you've applied.

Most government jobs follow a strict pay scale, available from the OPM as the General Schedule of salaries. (See next page.) Corporate lawyers, though, are in for a treat; the Federal Reserve Board and the Securities and Exchange Commission have a separate pay structure with higher wages. Most government attorneys start out at the GS-11 level ($41,684 in 2002), but promotions can make a big difference. A third-year GS-11, for instance, still had a base salary under $45,000 in 2002, but a GS-12 position boosts earnings to $53,000.

	STEP 1	STEP 2	STEP 3	STEP 4	STEP 5
GS-1	$14,757	$15,249	$15,740	$16,228	$16,720
GS-2	$16,592	$16,985	$17,535	$18,001	$18,201
GS-3	$18,103	$18,706	$19,309	$19,912	$20,515
GS-4	$20,322	$20,999	$21,676	$22,353	$23,030
GS-5	$22,737	$23,495	$24,253	$25,011	$25,769
GS-6	$25,344	$26,189	$27,034	$27,879	$28,724
GS-7	$27,164	$29,103	$30,042	$30,981	$31,920
GS-8	$31,191	$32,231	$33,271	$34,311	$35,351
GS-9	$34,451	$35,599	$36,747	$37,895	$39,403
GS-10	$37,939	$39,204	$40,469	$41,734	$42,999
GS-11	$41,684	$43,073	$44,462	$45,851	$47,240
GS-12	$49,959	$51,264	$53,289	$54,954	$56,619
GS-13	$59,409	$61,389	$63,369	$65,349	$67,329
GS-14	$70,205	$72,545	$74,885	$77,225	$79,565
GS-15	$82,580	$85,333	$88,086	$90,839	$93,592

	STEP 6	STEP 7	STEP 8	STEP 9	STEP 10
GS-1	$17,009	$17,492	$17,981	$18,001	$18,456
GS-2	$18,736	$19,271	$19,806	$20,341	$20,876
GS-3	$21,118	$21,721	$22,324	$22,927	$23,530
GS-4	$23,707	$24,384	$25,061	$25,738	$26,415
GS-5	$26,527	$27,285	$28,043	$28,801	$29,559
GS-6	$29,569	$30,414	$31,259	$32,104	$32,949
GS-7	$32,859	$33,798	$34,737	$35,676	$36,615
GS-8	$36,391	$37,431	$38,471	$39,511	$40,551
GS-9	$40,191	$41,339	$42,487	$43,635	$44,783
GS-10	$44,264	$45,529	$46,794	$48,059	$49,324
GS-11	$48,629	$50,018	$51,407	$52,796	$54,185
GS-12	$58,284	$59,949	$61,614	$63279	$64,944
GS-13	$69,309	$71,289	$73,269	$75,249	$77,229
GS-14	$81,905	$84,245	$86,585	$88,925	$91,265
GS-15	$96,345	$99,089	$101,851	$104,604	$107,357

Local governments

State and local governments are also serious recruiters of legal eagles. According to the U.S. Census, state and local governments employed approximately 400,000 judicial and legal personnel as of March 2001. (These positions aren't broken down by the Census Bureau and lawyers in other categories may not be counted.) Of course, municipal government recruiting is tricky because it can vary even within one state, but there are a few popular legal positions that have pretty standard hiring processes.

Trying to land a job with a district attorney's (DA) office can be as competitive as applying for an associate's position at a major law firm, especially in a large city. The three cities profiled in this guide – Chicago, Los Angeles and Manhattan – can (and often do) receive up to 20 times more applications than they have available positions, and put their prospective hires through as many as four separate interviews before making their final decision. Although the background checks aren't as extensive as for a federal position, a prosecutor's office will, at the very least, check an applicant's history for any criminal record and require a drug test.

This pattern holds in other large cities as well: the Bronx DA's office had more than 700 applicants to choose from in 2000, and made offers to just 55. Some attorney's offices have the resources to recruit on law school campuses, while others rely heavily on prospective candidates to show initiative and seek them out. Most, but not all, will have information about applying for employment on their web sites, although the smaller offices will often refuse to accept applications if they don't actually have a vacancy to fill. And some offices have their own unique setups, like the Miami-Dade County Attorney's office, which selects many of its new hires from participants in its summer clerk program, an internship available to five to eight students each year.

Guide to Nonprofit Recruiting

The legal teams at most nonprofit organizations have staff levels comparable to small or mid-level law firms – in a sense, they are boutique firms, just with much less lucrative practices. Some of the groups in this Guide have full-time staffs of a dozen people or less, and the primary legal duties might be handled by just one or two attorneys who spend as much, if not more, time managing research associates or coordinating pro bono volunteers as they do litigating or lobbying. Employment opportunities at these smaller organizations are usually few and far between, and even the larger groups have to choose new hires carefully to fit within their limited budget capabilities. So how do you get your foot in the door?

- Keep your eyes peeled for job announcements. Check the organization's web site frequently for new positions and vacancies. Be prepared to apply as soon as you learn that a suitable job has become available.

- If you can create a proposal that identifies a clear objective in line with a nonprofit's broader goals and outlines the steps you're prepared to take to achieve it, many groups will gladly sponsor your application for a one- to two-year fellowship from philanthropic institutions. In addition, larger nonprofits with generous donors, like the American Civil Liberties Union, are able to create their own fellowship programs.

- Consider a summer internship. The pay will be minimal at best, but you'll gain valuable experience in the field, and research or advocacy projects are often suitable for academic credit.

- Push your networking and schmoozing talents to their limits. If you're serious about working in a nonprofit's given field, chances are that you're already doing related work in your extracurricular activities. Grow your list of contacts. Make sure they know you're serious about your career plans, and don't be afraid to work them for a reference or introduction to somebody at your target organization.

EMPLOYER PROFILES

American Civil Liberties Union

125 Broad Street
18th Floor
New York, NY 10004
www.aclu.org

LOCATIONS

New York, NY (HQ)
Washington, DC
Atlanta, GA
Affiliated offices in every state

MAJOR DEPARTMENTS & PRACTICES

Criminal Justice
Cyber-Liberties
Death Penalty
Disability Rights
Drug Policy
Free Speech
HIV/AIDS
Immigrant Rights
Lesbian/Gay Rights
National Security
Police Practices
Prisons
Privacy
Racial Equality
Religious Liberty
Reproductive Rights
Students Rights
Voting Rights
Women's Rights
Workplace Rights

THE STATS

No. of attorneys: 55
President: Nadine Strossen
Legal Director: Steve Shapiro

BASE SALARY

1st year: $35,500-$37,000
(fellowship stipend "based on ACLU pay scale")

EMPLOYMENT CONTACT

http://www.aclu.org/jobs/jobsmain.cfm

THE SCOOP

Pacifist roots

The American Civil Liberties Union (ACLU) was established in 1920, an outgrowth of the National Civil Liberties Bureau, which had formed a few years earlier to help protect the rights of conscientious objectors to the United States' involvement in the First World War. Founding members included Roger Baldwin, a pacifist who had served time in prison for deliberately evading the draft, and feminist attorney and workers' rights advocate Crystal Eastman. Also lending their support were attorneys Clarence Darrow and Albert DeSilver, who provided the fledgling organization with much of its operating funds until his death in 1924, after which his widow continued to make annual donations in his name; today individuals who include the ACLU in their wills are granted memberships in the DeSilver Society.

One of the ACLU's earliest missions was organizing against the Justice Department's use of the Espionage Act and Sedition Act to arrest over 16,000 suspected communist and anarchist agitators, many of whom were held for months without trial. The ACLU mounted a similar effort for Japanese-Americans held in internment camps during World War II. Today the ACLU takes on cases it believes challenge the Bill of Rights, including cases regarding freedom of speech, separation of church and state, and criminal cases that involve unconstitutional arrest, detainment or punishment.

First, the First Amendment

One of the ACLU's main focuses is First Amendment cases. It challenged the Children's Internet Protection Act of 2000, which required public libraries with Internet access to install pornography-blocking filters. The organization claimed CIPA was too restrictive and would block library visitors access to legally protected speech. In June 2002, the 3rd U.S. Circuit Court agreed with the ACLU in American Library Association v. United States of America, declaring CIPA unconstitutional. The ACLU had brought the case on behalf of the library group as well as two organizations whose non-pornographic web sites were frequently blocked by filter software. In November 2002, the Supreme Court decided to review the case.

Other notable free speech cases in 2002 involved a suit against Pewaukee, Wis., over a city ordinance that bans homeowners from putting up political signs on their property until 45 days before an election; a suit against

Harborcreek Township, Penn., for demanding a candidate pay a $50 bond for each sign her supporters wanted to place on their lawns; and suits against two cities in Utah over laws that made hanging a "For Sale" sign in residents' cars illegal.

Losing my religion

The ACLU is well known for litigating cases related to the separation of church and state. In May 2002, the organization filed a lawsuit on behalf of Sean Shields, a math teacher in Plainview, Kan., who objected to the recitation of a prayer at the graduation ceremony for the town's school. That same month the organization filed a lawsuit challenging the Louisiana Governor's Abstinence Program, a program that promoted abstinence in public school sexual education classes. ACLU lawyers said the program amounted to a government promotion of religious beliefs, and cited a pamphlet linking increases in sexually transmitted diseases to the removal of prayer from public schools. In August 2002, the ACLU challenged a decision by the Cobb County, Ga., school board to introduce alternatives to the theory of evolution. The board inserted a disclaimer into the middle and high school texts stating that evolution is a theory and not fully established fact; the ACLU sued to have the school board reverse the policy. Also in August 2002, the Maryland chapter of the ACLU filed a lawsuit against the city of Frederick to force the removal of a large stone replica of the Ten Commandments.

The organization also presses for prisoners' rights. In April 2002, they filed suit against the Texas prison system on behalf of Roderick Johnson, arguing that prison administrators had "failed to take reasonable measures to prevent him from being victimized" by several prison gangs. Two months later, they advocated for a North Austin, Texas, teenager in a juvenile home who had been refused permission by a judge to leave the home temporarily to have an abortion.

Hanging chads banned in Cali

Thanks to an ACLU victory (one shared with other plaintiffs), Californians voting in the 2004 presidential elections won't have to worry about hanging chads. After the 2000 election debacle in Florida, California officials announced plans to replace their own punch-card voting machines with touch screens and optical scanners by July 2005, but the ACLU sued, saying that wasn't fast enough. U.S. District Judge Stephen V. Wilson agreed, though he wasn't as aggressive as the civil rights lawyers, who wanted new equipment installed by November 2002. Instead, California voters can look forward to new equipment in 2004.

Back where we started

In a series of cases reminiscent of those the group came together to fight, the ACLU has joined several lawsuits about detainees in the war on terrorism. ACLU lawyers have sued to force the government to reveal the names of foreign nationals arrested after the September 11 attacks and open their deportation hearings to the public. Although the ACLU and other groups have obtained several favorable rulings from judges who believed the Department of Justice did not sufficiently prove that keeping these cases under wraps was vital to national security, the government has appealed each of those decisions, in most cases delaying the release of the prisoners' names.

In another 9/11-related case, the ACLU helped file a discrimination suit in June 2002 against American Airlines, Continental Airlines, Northwest Airlines, and United Airlines on behalf of five men who claim they were ejected from flights because they looked "Middle Eastern."

GETTING HIRED

Check out the ACLU's web site, www.aclu.org, for job openings at the headquarters in New York, the national office in Washington, DC, or any of the regional offices across the country. You can also apply for several one-year fellowships that concentrate on areas such as cyberlaw or drug policy litigation. For example, third-year law students and recent law school graduates can apply for the organization's William J. Brennan First Amendment Fellowship. The fellowship, named after former Supreme Court Justice William Brennan, focuses on First Amendment and technology issues in the ACLU's headquarters in New York. Third-years and recent grads can also apply for the New York-based Marvin M. Karpatkin Fellowship in Civil Liberties. (The late Karpatkin was general counsel for the ACLU.) Other fellowships are available in the New York office for the Reproductive Freedom Project, the Lesbian and Gay Rights Project, and the ACLU AIDS Project. The application procedures for different fellowships vary slightly, but generally require a faxed or hard copy (no e-mail) application packet including a resume, references and a legal writing sample.

Central Intelligence Agency

Washington, DC 20505
Phone: (703) 482-0623
www.cia.gov

LOCATIONS

McLean, VA
Washington, DC

MAJOR DEPARTMENTS & PRACTICES

Center for the Study of Intelligence
Directorate of Intelligence
Directorate of Science and
    Technology
Directorate of Operations
Office of General Counsel
Office of Public Affairs

THE STATS

No. of attorneys: 100 (estimated;
actual numbers classified)
Director of Central Intelligence:
George J. Tenet
General Counsel: Scott Muller

BASE SALARY

1st year: $45,851 (GS-11/4)

THE SCOOP

Secret agent men

The Office of Strategic Services revolutionzed American military intelligence operations during World War II, but its sometimes loose administration drew much criticism from other branches of the government, and the agency was disbanded almost immediately after the war's end. The secret intelligence and counterintelligence divisions were absorbed into the War Department, and staffers from those bureaus would, after the passage of the National Security Act in 1947, form the nucleus of the Central Intelligence Agency (CIA). The agency's official functions are to coordinate intelligence gathered from operatives around the world, evaluate its relevance to U.S. security, conduct counterintelligence operations abroad and perform other covert operations at the direction of the President.

The Director of Central Intelligence is George Tenet, a Bill Clinton appointee. Tenet has years of intelligence experience, having served on the National Security Council and as staff director on the Senate Select Committee on Intelligence. Tenet – indeed, much of the intelligence and law enforcement community – came under scrutiny after the terrorist attacks of September 11, 2001 for lapses in security, but President George W. Bush has voiced support for the director, making an imminent change in CIA leadership unlikely.

Lawyers for spies

The CIA's Office of General Counsel advises the agency's director on legal matters relating to his position as the head of the CIA and, by extension, the "Intelligence Community" (which includes military intelligence and other government intelligence agencies). The office's 100 attorneys, all of whom have top secret clearance, can also provide legal advice to CIA officers pertaining to their specific responsibilities at the agency.

GETTING HIRED

The CIA has a comprehensive employment section on its web site, www.cia.gov, and prefers that you submit your resume electronically. Applicants must pass a strict background check, including polygraph tests, in order to obtain the necessary Top Secret security clearance. The agency offers summer law clerk positions for law students. Because the background check can take up to nine months to complete, summer applications must be in by the end of September of the preceding year. Summer interns are considered for full-time positions, but the CIA offers no guarantee that a clerk will be asked to stay.

The CIA also offers a two-year Legal Honors Program for exceptional law school grads. The first year is always at the CIA's Office of General Counsel. Second-years are sometimes placed in other government agencies with national security responsibilities like the Department of Justice or the National Security Agency.

The CIA offers a two-year Legal Honors Program for exceptional law school grads.

Cook County State's Attorney's Office

69 W. Washington Blvd.
Suite 3200
Chicago, IL 60602
Phone: (312) 603-5440
www.statesattorney.org

LOCATIONS

Chicago, IL and suburban locations

MAJOR DEPARTMENTS & PRACTICES

Civil Actions Bureau
Criminal Prosecutions Bureau
Juvenile Justice Bureau
Narcotics Prosecutions Bureau
Public Interest Bureau
Special Prosecutions Bureau

THE STATS

No. of attorneys: 900 +
State's Attorney: Richard A.
Devine

BASE SALARY

1st year: $41,548

EMPLOYMENT CONTACT

http://www.stateattorney.org/aweb/em
ploy.html

THE SCOOP

Giant of the Midwest

With 920 attorneys, the Cook County State's Attorney's Office has the second largest prosecuting team in the United States, just barely behind Los Angeles County. It operates in the country's largest unified court system, serving a county that stretches out over 1,000 square miles including the city of Chicago. In addition to the usual criminal and civil bureaus, the office has several special task forces that focus on prosecuting complex cases such as election fraud, gang-related activity and organized crime. It also maintains a Public Interest Bureau that prosecutes on behalf of defrauded consumers, seniors and persons with disabilities.

In February 2003, State's Attorney Richard A. Devine announced the formation of a new review program that would reexamine 100 murder convictions and consider the possibility of exonerating DNA evidence. The program bucks the trend of case reviews based on DNA evidence, which are usually initiated by defense attorneys. The previous year, DNA testing had cleared four men convicted of a 1985 murder and led investigators to two other suspects.

Cases in the news

R&B superstar R. Kelly was indicted in Cook County on June 5, 2002, on 21 counts of child pornography stemming from a videotape that depicted seven sexual acts between a man alleged to be Kelly and a female partner prosecutors say was a minor at the time the tape was made. Each of the acts carried a charge of enticing the girl to participate in the act, planning to videotape it, then actually videotaping it. Kelly was arrested in his Florida home before extradition to Chicago. He pled not guilty to all 21 counts, but was later indicted on similar charges in Florida.

Since its formation in 1999, the Cook's County State's Attorney's cold case squad has obtained 13 convictions in previously unsolved murders. In May 2002, they filed murder charges against two men in the 1993 "Brown's Chicken" massacre. Each of the seven victims had been taken into refrigerated coolers in the back of the fast-food restaurant and shot repeatedly. Although the two men claim that the murders were the result of a robbery gone wrong, prosecutors charge that the incident was thoroughly premeditated, though the alleged killers' motivation remains unknown. One was linked to the murder scene by DNA evidence from saliva on a discarded chicken bone; the ex-girlfriend of the other alleged perpetrator came forward after several years to report that he had bragged to her the night of the killings.

In August 2002, the cold case squad scored another major victory, landing the second set of convictions against Kenneth Hansen for the 1955 murder of three young boys. Although an earlier conviction had been overturned because of wrongfully introduced evidence of Hansen's pedophilic history, the second jury took less than four hours to determine Hansen's guilt in the triple homicide. He was resentenced in October to a minimum of 200 years.

Reining in the sheriff

In February 2002, a *Chicago Tribune* investigative piece revealed that state's attorneys had settled 32 cases charging brutality by deputies of the county sheriff's office over the previous four years, at a cost of $1.5 million, after concluding the cases would likely end in guilty verdicts because the department had falsified or "misplaced" documents and provided inconsistent accounts. The following month, however, a judge acquitted three officers in the beating death of Louis Schmude with just five minutes' deliberation, after having disparaged the prosecution and its witnesses repeatedly during proceedings, even walking out of the courtroom in disgust at one point.

GETTING HIRED

You'll find printable versions of the state's attorney's job application at the office's website, www.statesattorney.org, in PDF and Word formats. Recruiters for the office interview on over twenty law school campuses each fall, mostly within 100 miles of Chicago, though they do make it out to Washington, DC. You only need to be in the top half of your class, but writing for the law review or taking a courseload heavy in advocacy and criminal law will give you a good edge. If you get the job, expect to spend your first year in traffic court or prosecuting deadbeat dads for child support, but be prepared to take on more responsibility quickly.

If you get the job, expect
to spend your first year in
traffic court or prosecuting
deadbeat dads, but be
prepared to take on more
responsibility quickly.

DC Employment Justice Center

1350 Connecticut Ave. NW,
Suite 600
Washington, DC 20036
(202) 828-9675
www.dcejc.org

LOCATIONS

Washington, DC

MAJOR DEPARTMENTS & PRACTICES

Workers' Rights

THE STATS

No. of attorneys: 5
Director of Legal Services: Judith M. Conti

EMPLOYMENT CONTACT

E-mail: justice@dcejc.org
http://dcejc.org/jobs_&_internships.htm

THE SCOOP

The DC Employment Justice Center (DCEJC) was founded in September 2000 by Kerry O'Brien and Judith M. Conti, two DC-area lawyers with an interest in workers' rights. O'Brien and Conti received start-up funds from the Echoing Green Foundation, a New York-based philanthropic institution that finances "social entrepreneurs." The DCEJC provides legal assistance to about 120 low-income workers in the Washington metropolitan area each month, helping them resolve cases involving unpaid wages, unsafe working conditions, workplace discrimination and other employment law matters. Many of the center's clients get help at the regular Wednesday-night "Worker's Rights Clinic," consulting with lawyers, law students and paralegals who can advise them on how to resolve their problems.

In January 2002, the center launched the Program on Women's Employment Rights (POWER). The program, run in conjunction with the DC-based Wider Opportunities for Women, represents female low-income workers and has developed several fact sheets that explain women's rights in relation to topics like sexual harassment and the Family Medical Leave Act. The DCEJC also runs education programs that teach residents of the District's low-income communities (including those in welfare and workfare programs) about their employment rights.

In addition to working on individual cases, the center also advocates for changes within the system that will improve conditions for low-income workers. They participate in the DC Jobs Council, a coalition that seeks to make quality job training available on a more wide scale basis through the District, and the Welfare Advocates Group, which leads the fight to ensure "workfare" genuinely benefits the low-income workforce.

GETTING HIRED

The center sponsors several applicants for public interest law fellowships each year and recommends that you get your proposal in before the August 15 deadline to give you more time to work on the actual fellowship application, usually due in September or October. Check the center's web site, www.dcejc.org, which describes opportunities for internships and independent research and advocacy projects for which law students usually obtain academic credit; they also have a summer internship program.

Department of Agriculture

U.S. Department of Agriculture
1400 Independence Ave., SW
Washington, DC 20250
Phone: (202) 264-8600
www.usda.gov

LOCATIONS

Washington, DC (HQ)
5 regional offices, 13 branch
offices

THE STATS

No. of attorneys: 240
Secretary of Agriculture: Ann M.
Veneman

BASE SALARY

1st year: $48,451

EMPLOYMENT CONTACT

U.S. Department of Agriculture
Office of the General Counsel
Attention: Deborah Vita
1400 Independence Avenue, SW
Room 2041 - South Building
Washington, DC 20250

THE SCOOP

Farm livin' is the life for me

When President Lincoln created the Department of Agriculture (USDA) in 1862, 58 percent of the American population consisted of farming families and their employees. Today, only two percent of Americans are active farmers, but taken as a whole, agriculture is a trillion-dollar industry, representing 15 percent of the American gross national product. One-sixth of the national workforce makes a living from the food and fiber economy. The USDA continues to provide aid to farmers, but it also works to make sure all Americans have access to a safe, affordable food supply. And, though many people don't realize it, the USDA is responsible for the Forest Service, which has supervisory authority over 192 million acres of national forests and rangelands.

President George W. Bush appointed Ann Veneman as the 27th Secretary of Agriculture in January 2001, and she received unanimous approval from the Senate. Veneman, who grew up on a rural farm in California, first joined the USDA during the Reagan administration and served as Deputy Secretary under the first President Bush. She also ran the California Department of Food and Agriculture from 1995 to 1999.

Ad money

In 1985 the USDA began collecting assessments from pork and cattle producers and importers on the products they sell, with money designated for marketing and research programs. Similar "check-off" programs were later established for lamb and mohair producers and soybean farmers, and altogether the department was gathering $200 million a year in assessment fees. But the programs have been thrown into jeopardy by recent court rulings. In June 2002, the U.S. District Court in South Dakota ruled that the legislation creating the beef check-off program was unconstitutional and ordered the USDA to stop collecting assessments by July 15. The department received a stay on the ruling from the 8th Circuit Court of Appeals pending the outcome of the department's appeal. A judge in the District Court of Montana ruled in the USDA's favor in a similar case in October 2002, but just days before, the District Court in Michigan had struck down the pork check-off program on the grounds that it forced some pig farmers to subsidize advertising campaigns they did not support.

A 1999 settlement of a class-action lawsuit brought against the Department of Agriculture by thousands of black farmers charging discrimination over the department's denial of farm subsidy loans resulted in claims from nearly 23,000 farmers, far more than the government had expected. Although more than half of them have received compensation packages totaling $630 million, 40 percent of the applications have been rejected, and several angry farmers have agitated to get the settlement vacated if the USDA cannot enact its terms more efficiently.

GETTING HIRED

Click on the "employment opportunities" link at the USDA's web site, www.usda.gov, and you'll be redirected to the federal government's Office of Personnel Management, which provides a searchable list for each of the USDA's programs and divisions. Attorneys in the Office of General Counsel can work in the Washington headquarters and in regional offices around the country.

Attorneys in the Office of General Counsel can work in the Washington headquarters and in regional offices around the country.

Department of Commerce

U.S. Department of Commerce
1401 Constitution Avenue NW
Washington, DC 20230
Phone: (202) 482-2000
www.commerce.gov

LOCATIONS

Washington, DC

THE STATS

Secretary of Commerce: Donald L.
Evans
General Counsel: Theodore W.
Kassinger

EMPLOYEMENT CONTACT

http://www.commerce.gov/job.html

THE SCOOP

Everybody's business

The Department of Commerce, which celebrates its centennial in 2003, acts as the bridge between American businesses and the government. Secretary of Commerce Donald Evans, who was appointed head of the department by George W. Bush in 2001, describes his function on his home page as "working to create a climate in which the U.S. and global economies can grow." Perhaps the best way to describe the department's role is that it tries to ensure the American economy's smooth progress. It works with businesses to spur the development of new jobs and corporate growth. Specialized branches of the department concentrate on minority business development, technology administration, and international trade.

The Department of Commerce has performed a wide variety of services during its century of existence. It was originally named the Department of Commerce and Labor until Labor was spun off into its own Cabinet-level department in 1913, and fulfilled many of the functions that the Department of Transportation would take over in the 1960s. Two of the department's most important divisions, the Bureau of the Census and the U.S. Patent and Trademark Office, were both inherited from the Department of the Interior in 1903 and 1925, respectively. Commerce was also home to the forerunners of the Federal Aviation Administration and the Federal Communications Commission, both of which were launched under Herbert Hoover in the 1920s.

Gettin' fishy with it

The Department of Commerce has been involved in two cases involving fish stories. John Thompson, head of Louisiana's Delta Commercial Fisherman's Association, sued the Department in August 2002, claiming it had stacked the Gulf of Mexico Fishery Management Council with advocates of recreational fishing, in violation of a federal law mandating an equitable balance between recreational and commercial interests on the panel. The commerce secretary is responsible for appointing 11 of the panel's 17 members, who have substantial authority over fishing activities in the Gulf of Mexico.

At the same time, the department began a formal inquiry into charges that 14 members of the Vietnamese Association of Seafood Exporters and Processors (VASEP) had dumped tons of frozen catfish fillets onto the U.S. market, drastically undercutting American competition. The investigation marked the second phase of a lawsuit by the American Catfish Farmers Association against VASEP.

Counting to 288 million

The Census Bureau faced a number of lawsuits in the aftermath of the 2000 census. Utah failed to convince the Supreme Court that the bureau's guesstimates for several of the state's households were so low they cost the state a seat in the House of Representatives; state leaders also failed to get over 11,000 Mormon missionaries temporarily working overseas included in the tally. Several southern Californian cities, including Los Angeles, demanded that the bureau use statistical sampling techniques to adjust the data for their region, claiming that the raw data underrepresented the number of poor and minority residents, thus costing the cities billions of dollars in federal grant money. Their suit was rejected in April 2002; the 9th Circuit Court of Appeals upheld the dismissal in September. And the mayor of Whiteville, Tenn., prepared to sue over an error that placed the Whiteville Correctional Institution's 1,395 inmates outside the city, resulting in a loss of $138,746 in state-shared revenue.

GETTING HIRED

The Department of Commerce's web site, www.commerce.gov, has a section devoted to vacancy announcements and specific job information for some of its branches, including the Census Bureau and the National Oceanic and Atmospheric Administration. The department's Commerce Opportunities On-Line (COOL) system allows users to search for and apply to jobs online. Commerce jobs are also advertised by the Office of Personnel Management.

The Department of Commerce acts as a bridge between American businesses and the government.

Department of Education

U.S. Department of Education
400 Maryland Avenue, SW
Washington, DC 20202-0498
Phone: 800-USA-LEARN (800-872-5327)
www.ed.gov

LOCATIONS

Washington, DC
Boston, MA
New York, NY
Philadelphia, PA
Atlanta, GA
Chicago, IL
Dallas, TX
Kansas City, MO
Denver, CO
San Francisco, CA
Seattle, WA

MAJOR DEPARTMENTS & PRACTICES

(Within Office of General Counsel)
Postsecondary and Regulatory
   Service
Program Service
Departmental and Legislative
   Service

THE STATS

No. of other employees: 4,900
Secretary of Education: Rod Paige
General Counsel: Brian Jones

BASE SALARY

1st year: $45,744 (GS-11, Office of Civil Rights)

EMPLOYMENT CONTACT

http://www.ed.gov/offices/OM/edjobs.html

THE SCOOP

Teach the children well

Although the Department of Education has only been operational for just over two decades, the government's role in education dates as far back as the 1860s. The federal government first administered education through the Department of the Interior, and later via the Department of Health, Education, and Welfare (which was converted to Health and Human Services). The nation's concern with education accelerated in the late 1950s, as the space race highlighted the need for more science programs. Throughout the 1950s and 1960s, the government recognized a desire to improve educational services for people at all economic levels as well as racial minorities, women, people with disabilities, and non-English-speaking students. In the 1970s there was an increasing demand for a Cabinet-level agency, and Congress passed the Department of Education Organization Act in 1979.

According to their official web site, the Department "establishes policies relating to federal financial aid for education, administers distribution of those funds, and monitors their use" to ensure that all citizens can have access to educational resources without discrimination. In January 2002, the No Child Left Behind Act was signed into law. The statute is intended to hold America's public schools more accountable for the education they provide. One of the bill's major provisions allowed parents to transfer kids out of schools with consistently substandard performance levels, with the local schools picking up the tab for transportation to the new school. Board of Education officials in Richmond County, Ga., were among those who went to federal court seeking a one-year extension on the school choice option, arguing that they had insufficient time to implement a new busing plan. After receiving the extension, school superintendent Charles Larke met with Department of Education lawyers in late September 2002 to continue negotiations for the county's compliance with the law.

Title IX: Good sportswomanship

In 2002, the Department of Education became involved in several cases alleging violations of Title IX, a 1972 amendment to the Civil Rights Act that specifically bans gender-based discrimination in education. The National Women's Law Center filed petitions in all twelve of the Department's regional offices in June, contending that high school vocational programs throughout the country showed signs of discrimination by consistently training women for low-paying jobs. Male students were heavily enrolled in programs that could lead to industrial and technical careers, the petitions noted, and their eventual salaries could be as much as three times higher than those in the child care, cosmetology, or nursing jobs, for which most female vocational students were being trained.

Hammerlock on equality?

In one prominent Title IX case, the National Wrestling Coaches Association sued the Department of Education regarding its proportionality rule. The rule, established in 1979, requires schools to have a ratio of male to female athletes matching the overall ratio of male to female students. The NWCA's suit, filed in January 2002, claims the proportionality rule resulted in hundreds of colleges dropping men's wrestling to maintain gender balance in athletic programs. The Department of Justice, acting as Education's counsel, sought to have the case dismissed on procedural grounds, while voicing cautious support for the law itself. The Title IX statute may be undergoing some changes. The Bush administration assembled a Commission on Opportunities in Athletics to conduct hearings into the effects of Title IX on American colleges, leaving questions about the administration's ultimate stance on the law unresolved.

GETTING HIRED

The Department of Education's web site, www.ed.gov, has a full list of job openings, both for civil service positions and for competitive appointment positions (including attorneys). The department has special initiatives for diversity, including pushes for Hispanic candidates and candidates with disabilities. One current employee cautions, however, that the department generally seeks more experienced attorneys and only recruits at law schools for summer positions."

OUR SURVEY SAYS

The Department of Education's Office of General Counsel is a "warm, social environment." The work can generally be confined to a 40-hour week, which, as one attorney reports, "allows me to comfortably balance work with my personal life."

Employees describe a lack of formal training as a drawback to working at the department, though not an insurmountable one. "Fortunately, almost everyone here is very approachable," says one attorney, and colleagues are willing to help each other out. "Women are the majority" in the general counsel's office, and minority staffers say they "feel very welcome."

A potentially bigger problem stems from the cyclical nature of changing administrations, where political appointees often clash with career civil service workers. One Department of Education staffer suggests that the people brought on board by President Bush create a "sense of distrust and exclusitivity" that "has dramatically decreased the morale of the career employees."

Department of Energy

1000 Independence Avenue, SW
Washington, DC 20585
Phone: (800) 342-5363
www.energy.gov

LOCATIONS

Washington, DC

MAJOR DEPARTMENTS & PRACTICES

(Within Office of General Counsel)
Energy Policy
Environment and Nuclear Programs
General Law
Litigation
Office of Dispute Resolution
Technology Transfer
Procurement

THE STATS

No. of Attorneys: 110
Secretary of Energy: Spencer Abraham

THE SCOOP

Power to the people

The Department of Energy (DOE) was created in the first year of the Carter administration as a response to a nationwide fuel shortage during the unseasonably cold winter of 1977. The agency has four main goals: (1) the DOE oversees the nation's nuclear weapons and nuclear power programs; (2) in a similar vein, the agency monitors the disposal of nuclear and radioactive waste; (3) the department also runs an energy program that seeks to increase domestic energy production and promote conservation; (4) finally, the DOE's science program researches energy solutions, including alternative methods of production, and delivery of energy. The DOE is headed by Secretary of Energy Spencer Abraham, a George W. Bush appointee. Abraham is a Harvard Law graduate and a former United States senator from Michigan.

Energy production and conservation has always been a central concern of the department, but questions were raised in 2002 about how the Bush administration went about formulating its national energy policy. The General Accounting Office got most of the headlines by suing the White House when Vice President Dick Cheney refused to allow them access to documents related to the task force that wrote the policy. But a nonprofit environmental group, the Natural Resources Defense Council (NRDC), filed a suit against DOE seeking similar documents, after the department sat on a Freedom of Information Act request for nine months. U.S. District Judge Gladys Kessler ruled in the NRDC's favor in February 2002, ordering the department to release all documents pertaining to the DOE's involvement with Cheney's energy task force, including records of meetings with energy industry executives. The DOE eventually released approximately 1,000 pages of documents related to the task force.

Yucca Mountain morass

The DOE's nuclear waste disposal methods caused much controversy in 2002. The Nuclear Waste Policy Act of 1982 gave the department a mandate: find a single site that could serve as a repository for the entire country's spent nuclear fuel and hazardous waste, and established a fund for its construction into which the nation's nuclear plant owners would make regular payments. The federal government hoped to use space under Nevada's Yucca Mountain. Nevada resisted the idea of being the drop-off point for the country's nuclear waste, and fought the plans even after the White House authorized construction to begin in the summer of 2002.

The Act had originally required the government to complete a waste storage facility by 1998, but since Yucca Mountain was nowhere near ready, DOE was falling behind on contractual obligations to dispose of spent fuel from nuclear power plants across the country. The department had reached an agreement with Peco Energy (now a part of Exelon Corp.), whereby the department would take over Peco's waste but continue to store it at the company's plant while allowing Peco to offset contributions to the Yucca Mountain construction fund. A group of 18 rival utilities sued the government over that settlement, saying the arrangement gave Peco an unfair advantage by allowing it to reduce its waste costs. (Other nuclear facilities had to pay into the government waste fund while continuing to store waste at their own facilities.) The 11th U.S. Circuit Court of Appeals sided with the 18 angry nuclear firms in September 2002, saying that the fund was intended for only one purpose - building a facility at Yucca Mountain.

Plutonium fight

In the meantime, the federal government wanted to transfer six metric tons of weapons-grade plutonium from Colorado to South Carolina until it could be converted into fuel for nuclear power plants. South Carolina's governor, Democrat Jim Hodges, challenged the transfer, saying that the government hadn't run sufficient environmental studies, and charging that the administration was moving forward to help the re-election bid of a Republican Colorado senator. Hodges sued in federal court to stop the shipments (after threatening at one point to use state troopers to stop the shipments at the border). Two courts rejected the governor's case; in August 2002, while unconfirmed reports indicated that the shipments had begun, Hodges announced his intention to appeal to the U.S. Supreme Court.

GETTING HIRED

The DOE's web site, www.energy.gov, offers a wide assortment of career information including salary and benefits information and an online application process. Attorney positions are available at the department's Washington headquarters and at branch and affiliated offices.

Attorney positions are available at the Department of Energy's Washington headquarters and at branch and affiliated offices.

Department of Health and Human Services

200 Independence Avenue, S.W.
Washington, DC 20201
Phone: (202) 619-0257
www.hhs.gov

LOCATIONS

(OGC offices)
Washington, DC
Baltimore, MD
Bethesda, MD
Rockville, MD.
Atlanta, GA
Boston, MA
Chicago, IL
Dallas, TX
Denver, CO
Kansas City, MO
New York, NY
Philadelphia, PA
San Francisco, CA
Seattle, WA

MAJOR DEPARTMENTS & PRACTICES

(within Office of General Counsel)
Business and Administrative Law
Children, Families, and Aging
Civil Rights
Ethics
Food and Drug
Health Care Financing
Legislation
Public Health

THE STATS

No. of attorneys: 345 (OGC)
No. of other employees: 67,000 (approximate)
Secretary of Health and Human Services: Tommy G. Thompson
General Counsel: Alex Michael Azar II

EMPLOYMENT CONTACT

http://www.hhs.gov/jobs/index.html

THE SCOOP

HHS likes Ike

One of Dwight Eisenhower's first acts as president upon taking office in 1953 was to authorize the creation of the Department of Health, Education and Welfare (HEW). In 1979, after a Cabinet-level department was created specifically to deal with education, HEW was renamed the Department of Health and Human Services (HHS). The department manages more than 300 programs related to medical and other basic services. Secretary of Health and Human Services Tommy Thompson, a graduate of the University of Wisconsin's law school, was appointed head of the department by George W. Bush. He was in the middle of his fourth term as governor of Wisconsin when he took office in January 2001.

One of the department's most well known functions is its administration of Medicare and Medicaid. Medicare alone is the nation's largest health care provider, processing 900 million claims a year for 39 million elderly and disabled Americans, while Medicaid, which the federal government runs in cooperation with the states, serves 34 million low-income citizens annually. HHS's Medicare and Medicaid administration does lead to the occasional courtroom appearance. The Michigan Department of Community Health launched a "preferred drug program" in February 2002, allowing the state's Medicaid recipients easier access to certain prescription drugs on a preferred list – including several medications made by pharmaceutical firms who gave the state rebates in order to get on the list. The Pharmaceutical Research and Manufacturers of America (PhRMA), an industry trade group, sued the HHS to force it to withdraw its approval for the program, claiming it was unconstitutional and would supply Michigan Medicaid patients with inferior drugs. Similar programs are in the works in 11 other states; a loss for the HHS would cancel those programs. But a December 2002 ruling in a related lawsuit, filed by PhRMA in Michigan's state court system, which declared the health plan legal, set a possible precedent for the federal case, on which a decision was expected in early 2003.

The department also investigates, through the inspector general's office, cases of Medicare and Medicaid fraud. HHS settled with the Eagle Point School District of Oregon in June 2002 for $1.2 million in damages, restitutions, and fines stemming from a five-year period of fraudulence. Schools in the district filed Medicaid claims for student health care services that were improperly documented, didn't qualify for reimbursement, or simply never took place.

Adding insult to injury, at least one employee represented himself to other school districts as an expert in Medicaid billing, charging the districts a percentage of the reimbursements they got from the government using his techniques.

In August 2002, three Medicare patients, backed by several special interest groups, sued the department to force it to streamline its process for appealing coverage denials. The three patients, suffering from a disease that causes casual blindness, were denied coverage for a treatment HHS deemed "experimental." Congress mandated that HHS streamline its appeals process but the department missed an October 1, 2001 deadline.

The HHS inspector general's office investigated the possible misuse of a federal research grant at Duke University's Center for Demographic Studies. Two of the center's former employees, Edward Davison and Christopher Fowler, were fired in 2001 after being charged with theft for using a Duke credit card to buy restaurant equipment for a diner they leased in nearby Roxboro. That proved to be only the tip of the iceberg, however, and Duke agreed in August 2002 to return $682,000 to HHS' National Institute on Aging. (Davison and Fowler, meanwhile, skipped bail on the theft charges and remain at large.)

GETTING HIRED

The department maintains a list of vacancy announcements on its web site at www.hhs.gov, sorted by agency. You can also go through the federal government's Office of Personnel Management web site at www.usajobs.opm.gov.

OUR SURVEY SAYS

"The culture at HHS can be somewhat formal," says one attorney, but there are also plenty of opportunities for socializing with colleagues, from bowling parties with the General Counsel to cultural events celebrating the traditions of African-American and Latino employees. "Though suits are preferred," she adds, "business casual wear is never frowned upon;" just don't show up for work in jeans, even on Fridays. The legal department is heavily staffed with female attorneys, including several in top-ranking positions, and sources attest to a "fair" mix of ethnic backgrounds as well.

Department of Housing and Urban Development

451 7th Street SW
Washington, DC 20410
Phone: (202) 708-1112
www.hud.gov

LOCATIONS

Washington, DC
Other offices nationwide

THE STATS

No. of Attorneys: 19 (within Office
of General Counsel)
**Secretary of Housing and Urban
Development:** Mel Martinez
General Counsel: Richard A. Hauser

EMPLOYMENT CONTACT

Esther L. Pigg
esther.l.pigg@hud.gov
http://www.hud.gov/jobs/index.cfm

THE SCOOP

A roof over your head

Lyndon Johnson consolidated several preexisting federal housing agencies into the Cabinet-level Department of Housing and Urban Development (HUD) in 1965. The department addresses the housing needs of American citizens through a variety of programs. The Federal Housing Authority helps over a million families each year purchase their first home by providing mortgage home insurance. More than 4.3 million low-income families participate in HUD's public housing or rent subsidy programs. And nearly 4,000 cities and counties use Community Development Block Grants to make improvements to housing or public facilities and support the growth of local businesses.

President Bush's HUD Secretary, Mel Martinez, was chairman of Florida's Orange County and had served on the Orlando Housing Authority. A Cuban refugee brought to America as a child by a Catholic humanitarian group in 1962, Martinez was a major supporter of Bush's faith-based initiative proposal and launched a center within HUD to cooperate with faith-based and community programs soon after taking office.

Fighting markup fees

U.S. Attorneys and HUD lawyers filed amicus briefs in three 2002 class-action lawsuits brought by homeowners who were charged excessive markup fees during their mortgage settlements – for example, $450 for an appraisal that only cost the lender $20 to obtain. The government has long maintained that charging such "unearned" fees is a violation of the 1974 Real Estate Settlement Procedures Act, but a judge in the 4th and 7th Circuit Courts of Appeals disagreed, ruling that the consumer protection law did not have sufficient strong language to support the federal markup ban. In response, HUD filed briefs in three separate cases in the 8th and 11th Circuits, as well as another 7th Circuit case, hoping to bring about a contradictory ruling that would essentially require the Supreme Court to resolve the discrepancy.

Throw 'em out

In March 2002, the Supreme Court accepted a HUD regulation that allowed public housing administrators to evict tenants whose relatives or associates engaged in illegal drug activity, even if they did so without the permission or even the knowledge of the actual leaseholder. The law had been challenged by several elderly Oakland residents who had been threatened with eviction from their apartments because their children or grandchildren – and, in one case, a live-in caretaker – had been caught with drugs on or near the property. The 9th Circuit Court of Appeals had ruled in favor of the tenants, finding the HUD policy "absurd," noting that property owners with no prior knowledge of illegal drug activity by family members or associates were exempt from government seizure of their assets, but the Supreme Court decided in an 8-0 vote that when the government acts as a public housing landlord, it has the right to control the activities of its tenants. (Justice Stephen Breyer recused himself because his brother, a federal judge, had made a ruling in the case back in 1998.)

With the cooperation of the Department of Justice, HUD filed a discrimination lawsuit against the Cypress Gardens Condominium Association of Hollywood, Fla., accusing the group of violating the Fair Housing Act. The suit stemmed from a 1998 complaint filed with HUD by condo owner Winston Mieli and Yves Belot, an African-American accountant to whom Mieli had wanted to rent. At first, the condo association claimed that Belot's rental application was incomplete, but continued to stonewall no matter how many details subsequent applications provided. At one point, Mieli simply gave Belot permission to move into the one-bedroom unit; the association swiftly responded with an eviction notice. The case is pending.

A rebuilding gets the OK

HUD successfully deflected a legal challenge to a redevelopment project in Seattle, Wash. The department, along with the Seattle Housing Authority, planned to demolish 481 low-income housing units in the Rainier Vista project to make room for 1,010 new units. Lawyers for the Seattle Displacement Coalition sued HUD and the Seattle Housing Authority because the new project would only have 410 low-income units. The housing authority argued that it would provide units elsewhere in the city to make up the difference. In October 2002, a court denied the Seattle Displacement Coalition's request for an injunction and allowed the project to continue.

GETTING HIRED

Although HUD does have some career information at its web site, www.hud.gov, it primarily refers potential applicants to the searchable job databases maintained by the government's Office of Personnel Management. One notable exception is HUD's Office of the Inspector General, which is aggressively looking for qualified applicants to fill auditing and criminal investigation positions and hires lawyers for its general counsel staff.

Department of the Interior

1849 C Street NW
Washington, DC 20240
Phone: (202) 208-3100
www.interior.gov

LOCATIONS

Washington, DC (HQ)
Albuquerque, NM
Anchorage, AK
Atlanta, GA
Billings, MT
Boise, ID
Boston, MA
Denver, CO
Minneapolis/St. Paul, MN
Palm Springs, CA
Phoenix, AZ
Pittsburgh, PA
Portland, OR
Sacramento, CA
Salt Lake City, UT
San Francisco, CA
Santa Fe, NM
Tulsa, NM

THE STATS

No. of attorneys: 340
(approximately 300 attorneys in
the DOI's Solicitor's Office and
about 30 or 40 attorneys in the
rest of the department)
No. of other employees: 70,000+
Secretary of the Interior: Gale
Norton
Solicitor: William G. Myers III

EMPLOYMENT CONTACT

For Solicitor's Office
http://www.doi.gov/sol and
http://www.usajobs.opm.gov

BASE SALARY

1st year: $41, 684 (GS-11); attorneys
can rise to $70,205 (GS-14)

THE SCOOP

Department of flora and fauna

The Department of the Interior traces its roots back to 1849, when Congress created the agency, also known at the time as the Home Department. Interior managed a wide variety of affairs, including exploring newly acquired territories in the West and maintaining the District of Columbia's water system. Some functions, including education and the Patent Office, have been made separate Cabinet departments or part of other divisions. Now the Department of the Interior manages the nation's natural resources and national parks; the Bureau of Indian Affairs maintains relations with the country's various Native American tribes. The Department of the Interior is headed by Secretary Gail Norton, a graduate of University of Denver's law school. Prior to her appointment by George W. Bush, Secretary Norton served as attorney general of Colorado and as associate solicitor for the Department of the Interior.

The department is a frequent target for those who believe the government isn't doing enough to protect the environment. In February 2002, for example, a coalition of conservation groups filed a lawsuit against the department and the U.S. Fish and Wildlife Service (FWS), which is managed by Interior, demanding that they place the mountain plover on the endangered species list. Endangered status for the plover, a small bird once found throughout the Great Plains, was originally proposed in 1999, and was supposed to have been resolved within a year. FWS blames the delay on the sheer number of requests and related lawsuits but, in a settlement negotiated by the nonprofit environmental law firm Earthjustice, agreed to expedite proceedings on the mountain plover proposal and reach a decision by September 2003.

This land is your land

Earthjustice also filed a lawsuit against Interior in April 2002, challenging ten of Interior Secretary Gale Norton's appointments to advisory councils that make recommendations to the department's Bureau of Land Management (BLM) concerning public lands in Colorado. The suit alleges that Norton's appointees in 2001, rather than reflecting the full spectrum of public land interests, benefited from political handouts by Colorado Governor Bill Owens; it further alleged that his recommendation list was sent in incompletely prepared nearly two weeks past deadline, but still prevailed over fifty other qualified applicants. Earthjustice sought to have the appointments overturned and establish new guidelines that would prevent such an incident from reoccurring.

In March 2002, Interior officials reached a settlement with New Mexico-based river advocacy group Amigos Bravos, which filed a lawsuit when BLM issued a permit to Taos Gravel Products, Inc., for a gravel mine less than a mile from the Rio Grande, an alleged violation of the Wild and Scenic Rivers Act. The settlement called for a complete shutdown of the mine, removal of all the equipment, and full restoration of the 42 acres on which the mine had operated.

A 100-year-old grievance

The Interior Department Bureau of Indian Affairs (BIA) is one of the nation's oldest federal agencies, predating even the department itself. (It started out as a branch of the War Department in 1824.) In 1887, when Congress appropriated 90 million acres of Native American Indian territory for white homesteaders, it established a fund that would provide the tribes with royalties collected through the department's management of grazing, timber and oil and grass drilling rights on the land. The fund was never properly managed, however, and in 1996 a group of tribal leaders sued the government for their unpaid royalties, which were estimated at anywhere between $10 billion and $40 billion. The suit dragged on for years, and the second phase of its trial didn't begin until January 2002. Later that year, U.S. District Judge Royce Lamberth cited Secretary Norton for contempt over the department's failure to obey court orders to fix the trust fund's oversight problems in a timely manner. (Three years earlier, after the trial's first phase, he'd made a similar judgment against the heads of both the Interior and the Treasury departments.) Writing that "there is no longer any doubt that the secretary of interior has been and continues to be an unfit trustee-delegate for the United States," Lamberth indicated that he might even appoint an outside trust expert to take over the fund's administration.

GETTING HIRED

You have to dig deep to find the employment information on the Department of the Interior's web site, www.interior.gov (look for the Office of Human Resources in the list of Bureaus/Offices). Once you're there, you can find links to the job sites for several DOI agencies, including the U.S. Fish and Wildlife Service and the Bureau of Land Management. The site also has a list of benefits and a description of its intern program. Interior job vacancies are usually filled through the federal Office of Personnel Management.

For the department's Solicitor's Office, where the majority of attorneys with the department are employed, job openings can be found at http://www.doi.gov/sol and http://www.usajobs.opm.gov. The department only responds to applications related to open positions at the sites listed above. The department does not respond to unsolicited applications.

Department of Justice

950 Pennsylvania Avenue, NW
Washington, DC 20530
Phone: (202) 353-1555
www.justice.gov

LOCATIONS

Washington, DC

MAJOR DEPARTMENTS & PRACTICES

Antitrust
Civil
Civil Rights
Criminal
Environment and Natural Resources
Executive Office for Immigration
    Review
Federal Bureau of Prison
Tax
U.S. Attorney

THE STATS

No. of attorneys: 9,200
No. of other employees: 134,000 +
Attorney General: John Ashcroft

BASE SALARY

1st year: $41,684

EMPLOYMENT CONTACT

Job Information Line: (202) 514-3396
http://www.justice.gov/06employment
/index.html

THE SCOOP

To enforce the law

Although the Attorney General's post was established in 1789 to represent the government in legal matters and advise the executive branch, it wasn't until 1870 that Congress created a Justice Department to assist him in that role and in the enforcement of federal laws. Today the U.S. Attorney's office prosecutes federal cases through six divisions that cover antitrust cases, civil lawsuits, civil rights violations, federal crimes, environmental law, and tax cases. (The department also encompasses many law enforcement agencies; like the Federal Bureau of Investigation and the Immigration and Naturalization Service.)

Attorney General John Ashcroft is the head of the Justice Department. Ashcroft received his JD from the University of Chicago. He served as attorney general and governor of Missouri as well as U.S. senator from that state before being named attorney general by George W. Bush.

Fighting terror

Congress and President Bush have given the Justice Department far-reaching authority to fight terrorism within the nation's borders. The Justice Department has made full use of those sometimes-controversial powers. The department has detained those suspected of links to terrorism for extended periods without filing charges and closed the deportation hearings of arrested foreign citizens in the interest of national security. Some civil rights organizations have challenged these practices and have filed suits to open hearings and force more disclosure on matters related to the detainment of suspects.

The department also began to prosecute high profile cases against accused terrorists and terrorist supporters. Zacarias Moussaoui is the only defendant thus far charged with direct involvement in the September 11 attacks; the six counts of criminal conspiracy include his plans to commit aircraft piracy, to destroy aircraft, to murder government employees and to destroy property. John Walker Lindh, an American citizen who was captured alongside other Taliban fighters in Afghanistan, was charged with ten separate counts but pled guilty in July to supplying services to the Taliban while carrying explosives and was sentenced to 20 years in federal prison. Richard Reid, the "shoe bomber" who tried to blow up a transatlantic flight in December 2001, pled guilty in October to all eight counts against him (despite his refusal to acknowledge the legitimacy of the American justice system).

Busting bad guy CEOs

The department has also been working overtime to fight corporate crime, going after former executives of the Houston-based energy firm Enron with a vengeance. Federal prosecutors scored victory in May 2002 with a guilty verdict in the obstruction of justice trial of accounting firm Arthur Andersen for its handling of Enron's finances. In August 2002, Justice announced former managing director Michael Kopper pled guilty to a criminal indictment that alleged that he and several co-conspirators worked to hide Enron's losses and risks through phony off-balance-sheet companies. His statement led to the October 2002 arrest of CFO Andrew Fastow on charges of security fraud, money laundering, mail fraud, wire fraud and bank fraud plus conspiracy related to each offense.

In July 2002, the president authorized the creation of a special corporate fraud task force within the Justice Department, with additional input from the Department of Treasury, the Securities and Exchange Commission and three other agencies. In the task force's first three months of operations, the department filed charges against more than 150 people. One of the task force's first successes was a guilty plea in September 2002 from three Homestore.com executives to securities fraud, wire fraud, and insider trading. Days later, WorldCom's former controller admitted his part in falsifying the telecommunication company's financial records to overstate profits by as much as $7 billion, followed by ex-accounting director Buford Yates. Both men stated that they were acting under orders from senior executives at the firm.

Hang 'em high

When John Muhammad and Lee Malvo were arrested in late October 2002 as suspects in a series of sniper shootings in Virginia and Maryland, authorities knew they would have to sift through conflicting jurisdictional concerns. Perhaps because the killings took place practically in the department's backyard, the Attorney General's office took a strong interest in the case and cut to the head of the prosecutorial line by filing a capital extortion charge against Muhammad. (Federal charges against Malvo were not discussed publicly because of his status as a minor.) But after a week's deliberation, they dropped the charge and transferred the two into the custody of Virginia, widely considered to have, in Ashcroft's words, "the best law, the best facts, and the best range of available penalties" – i.e., the best chance for a successful death penalty conviction.

Fighting for civil rights

In one of the year's biggest civil rights cases, Justice attorneys reached a settlement in April 2002 with the police department of Cincinnati, Ohio, which had been accused of using racial profiling to target its African-American citizens, 17 of whom had been killed in confrontations with police between 1995 and 2001. The agreement was integrated with the settlement of a lawsuit filed against the city by the American Civil Liberties Union and a local African-American organization. Cincinnati's law enforcement officials agreed to establish firm policies on foot pursuits and the use of chemical spray while apprehending suspects, as well as department-wide training on responding to calls involving the mentally ill. (One of the shooting victims was a mentally ill man who had threatened officers with a brick.)

Smokin'

In 1999 the Clinton administration launched a civil lawsuit against several tobacco companies, charging them with fraud, racketeering, and conspiracy to conceal the health risks of smoking. Though many were concerned when John Ashcroft called for settlement talks soon after taking over the department, Justice's proposed terms, released in March 2002, would impose the severest restrictions yet on the industry. The government's demands include a complete ban on vending-machine sales and give-away promotions and sharp limits on the types of advertising in which tobacco companies could engage. Cigarette manufacturers would also be required to devote 50 percent of their product's packaging to "graphic" health warnings, as well as include leaflets "created and supervised by the U.S. Surgeon General" inside every pack. The trial is scheduled to begin in June 2003.

GETTING HIRED

The Department of Justice runs its own Office of Attorney Recruitment and Management and offers information about hiring guidelines through its web site, www.justice.gov. The U.S. Attorney's office hires only experienced attorneys. Less experienced lawyers, including third-year law students and judicial clerks, can apply to the Attorney General's Honors Program. Honors applications are accepted through the department's web site and only for a limited time from early August through late September. Candidates should have good grades and law review experience, and volunteer or work experience that matches the department's functions.

Eight of the Justice Department's units (antitrust, civil, civil rights, environment and natural resources, tax, the Federal Bureau of Prison, the Executive Office for Immigration Review and the Immigration and Naturalization Service) hire summer law interns. (The U.S. Attorney does not.) Applicants must have at least one semester of law school under their belt. Like the Honors Program, applications must be submitted online by a specific date in late September.

Less experienced lawyers, including third-year law students and judicial clerks, can apply to the Attorney General's Honors Program.

Department of Labor

Frances Perkins Building
200 Constitution Avenue, NW
Washington, DC 20210
Phone: (866) 487-2365
www.labor.gov

LOCATIONS

Washington, DC

THE STATS

No. of attorneys: 500
No. of other employees: 17,483
Secretary of Labor: Elaine L. Chao
Acting Solicitor: Howard M.
Radzely

BASE SALARY

1st year: $47,910

EMPLOYMENT CONTACT

http://www.labor.gov/oasam/doljobs/
main.htm

THE SCOOP

Taft's last acts

William Howard Taft signed the law creating the Department of Labor in his last hours as President, just before Woodrow Wilson took office in March 1913. The new department, intended to "foster, promote and develop the welfare of the wage earners of the United States," was assembled from four existing government agencies that dealt with statistics, immigration, naturalization and child welfare, plus a new labor mediation group, the U.S. Conciliation Service. (Only the Bureau of Labor Statistics remains within the department today.) The department is responsible for enforcing over 180 federal laws pertaining to labor-related issues, including regulations that deal with the minimum wage (Fair Labor Standards Act), the 12-week maternity leave requirement (the Family and Medical Leave Act) and a law that bans forced polygraphs for most employees (the Employee Polygraph Protection Act).

They work hard for the money

The department often takes legal action on behalf of wronged employees. In May 2002, poultry processor Perdue farms agreed to a $10 million settlement with the Department of Labor. Perdue had not paid over 25,000 workers for the time spent every day putting on and taking off special equipment needed for their work, including earplugs and lab coats, saying the minutes spent "donning and doffing" were similar to other, non-compensated prep time. The company relented and agreed to pay back wages and to change its policy. Tyson Foods, a Perdue competitor, is facing a similar federal lawsuit by the department but has refused to settle. That case is pending.

In October 2002, Labor reached an agreement with the Coca-Cola Company after a review by the Office of Federal Contract Compliance Programs (OFCCP) determined that the soft drink manufacturer had practiced compensation discrimination against 922 female salaried employees, as well as 48 minority workers on hourly wages. In addition to $4.2 million in backpay compensation and over $900,000 in prospective salary adjustments, the settlement also called upon Coca-Cola to strengthen its commitment to equal employment opportunity and bring them in line with the standards required of all companies doing business with the federal government.

Crooked E

The department also had a hand in the government's continuing probe into the circumstances behind Enron's bankruptcy because of the way the company's collapse affected employee pension plans. In August 2002, four months after successfully negotiating with Enron to have State Street Bank & Trust manage what was left of the pension funds, lawyers for the department filed an amicus curiae brief in a class action lawsuit by former and current Enron employees. Labor asserted that, if the allegations in the complaint were true, the company's executives (including former CEO Ken Lay) could be held personally liable under the Employee Retirement Income Security Act for the mismanagement that caused the funds, which relied heavily on Enron stock, to collapse.

GETTING HIRED

The Department of Labor's web site, www.labor.gov, has a detailed employment section that includes career opportunities for lawyers and criminal investigators at various branches in the department.

The Department of Labor often takes legal action on behalf of wronged employees.

Department of State

2201 C Street NW
Washington, DC 20520
Phone: (202) 647-4000
www.state.gov

LOCATIONS

Washington, DC

THE STATS

No. of attorneys: 130
No. of other employees: 5,000
(United States)
Secretary of State: Colin Powell
Legal Adviser: William H. Taft IV

EMPLOYMENT CONTACT

**Office of Recruitment, Examination
and Employment**
United States Department of State
HR/REE, SA-1
2401 E Street, NW, 5H
Washington, DC 20522
Phone: (202) 261-8888
Fax: (202) 261-8841
http://www.state.gov/employment/

THE SCOOP

America's ambassador to the world

The State Department administrates the government's diplomatic relations with foreign countries – in fact, the 1789 legislation creating the department called it the Department of Foreign Affairs. Congress passed follow-up legislation later that summer renaming the department and granting it some additional duties, including custody of the Great Seal of the United States, which is stamped on treaty proclamations and letters of appointment for all U.S. ambassadors. Thomas Jefferson became the nation's first Secretary of State in 1790, as well as the first of six secretaries who would later move into the Oval Office.

Secretary of State Colin Powell is the 65th person to hold the position. Appointed by President George W. Bush, Powell was a professional soldier who rose to the rank of four-star general in the U.S. Army. Powell was chairman of the Joint Chiefs of Staff from 1989 through 1993 and led the victorious U.S.-led coalition in the Persian Gulf War. Most recently, he served as chairman at America's Promise - the Alliance for Youth, a nonprofit organization based in Alexandria, Va., that "build[s] the character and competence of our nation's youth," according to its web site.

A department that speaks legalese

The Office of the Legal Adviser counsels State Department officials on domestic and international legal issues that arise in the implementation of its foreign policy. The office's 130 attorneys help in the drafting of international agreements, the interpretation of federal legislation and executive orders, and frequently represent the department at international conferences and in United Nations programs. It has five regional divisions covering international law around the world and 18 functional offices that specialize in areas such as the nonproliferation of weapons of mass destruction, human rights, and extradition to or from foreign countries.

The Office of War Crimes Issues has a globe-spanning assignment that requires its staff to travel overseas on a regular basis, with frequent visits to the international courts at the Hague as well as trouble spots in the Balkans and Africa. The office is run by an ambassador-at-large who keeps the Secretary of State apprised of U.S. participation in the efforts to hold accountable perpetrators of war crimes and other crimes against humanity. In recent years, it has been the coordinating office for U.S. support of the International Criminal Tribunals for Rwanda and the former Yugoslavian republics.

GETTING HIRED

The State Department's web site, www.state.gov, lists open positions in various departments, including foreign service officers and specialists and in the Office of Civil Rights. You'll also find information for internships. The Office of the Legal Adviser hires second-year law students as summer interns and second- and third-years for fall and spring semester internships. The Office of the Inspector General hires second-year law students into its internship program.

The Office of the Legal Adviser hires second-year law students as summer interns.

Department of the Treasury

1500 Pennsylvania Avenue NW
Washington, DC 20220
Phone: (202) 622-1260
www.treasury.gov

LOCATIONS

Washington, DC

MAJOR DEPARTMENTS & PRACTICES

Banking and Finance
Enforcement
General Law and Ethics
International Affairs

THE STATS

No. of attorneys: 1,600
No. of other employees: 160,000
Secretary of the Treasury: John W. Snow
General Counsel: David Aufhauser

BASE SALARY

1st year: $46,469 (ATF attorney, GS-11)

EMPLOYMENT CONTACT

Jeanne Ramsey
Phone: (202) 622-0301
Jeanne.Ramsey@do.treas.gov
http://www.treas.gov/offices/general-counsel

THE SCOOP

Making money since 1787

The Constitution provides for a treasury to compensate members of Congress and for other government expenditures. In September 1789, Congress codified the Department of the Treasury's functions and defined the duties of the Secretary of the Treasury. The department still carries out many of its original functions but has also taken on several addition responsibilities in more than two centuries of operation. Although the U.S. Mint began producing coins in 1792, the Bureau of Engraving and Printing didn't start producing a standardized paper currency until 1862. The Bureau of Internal Revenue, forerunner of the IRS, was also created that year to collect income taxes to finance the Civil War. It enforced Prohibition during the 1920s because the Bureau of Alcohol, Tobacco, and Firearms wasn't created until 1972. The Secret Service also has its origins in the Civil War era, when its primary responsibility was to combat the widespread distribution of counterfeit versions of the new standardized national currency and it took on the responsibility of guarding government officials in 1901, after the assassination of President William McKinley, because at the time it was the government's law enforcement agency.

President George W. Bush appointed Secretary of the Treasury Paul O'Neill in early 2001. O'Neill served as chairman and CEO of Alcoa and president of International Paper before taking the post as head of the Department of Treasury. His tenure began in controversy, when he initially refused to divest himself of $100 million in Alcoa stock, and his contrarian reactions to the deepening economic recession failed to assuage critics. After nearly two years of service, he resigned so abruptly in December 2002 that he was already out of town by the time the press was notified of his decision. After a weekend's deliberation, Bush selected John Snow, the head of railroad holding company CSX, to fill the vacancy, a decision unlikely to be challenged when the now Republican-controlled Senate reconvened.

Hitting the enemy's wallet

The Treasury's Office of Enforcement, through the Office of Foreign Asset Control (OFAC), enforces economic and trade sanctions the government imposes against foreign nations. The OFAC that prosecutes individuals and businesses for violating the Trading With the Enemy Act by engaging in trade with banned nations like Cuba, North Korea and Iraq. OFAC also enforces bans on trade with individuals and organizations identified as "specially designated nationals" (SDNs) who do business on behalf of those nations or, increasingly, terrorist organizations, and seizes the assets of SDNs within America's borders.

The Treasury Department made extensive use of that power, plus broader powers provided by President Bush's Executive Order 13224, in the months following September 11, freezing the assets of several entities believed to have financial links to terrorism. The department claims to have seized $34.3 million in terrorist assets since September 11, 2001 as of November 2002. In one high-profile case, the Texas-based Holy Land Foundation, which had raised $13.3 million in 2000 for various Palestinian causes, was shut down by the department, based on FBI reports that they had extensive ties to the terrorist group Hamas. The foundation attempted to regain control of its assets with a federal lawsuit, but the suit was dismissed in August 2002. A federal court determined that the government had supplied substantial evidence of ties between the two groups.

Money for the blind

If the American Council for the Blind gets its way, the recent redesign of most of our paper currency won't be the last. The group filed suit in May 2002, based on a 1973 law that prohibits the government from denying disabled Americans the benefits of participating in any federal program or activity. The council's suit argues that the uniform dimensions of the larger-denomination bills designed by the Bureau of Engraving and Printing prevent people with visual disabilities from fully participating in many kinds of cash transactions. The group offered several possible alternatives, including the use of Braille markings or different-sized currency notes.

Fighting a glass ceiling

Two separate bureaus of the Treasury faced discrimination charges in 2002. A group of black AFT agents filed a motion in March 2002, arguing that the department had not implemented the personnel reforms mandated in a discrimination settlement six years earlier. Just over a month later, Hispanic Customs agents initiated a new suit alleging nearly 30 years of discriminatory practices. Eight agents, claiming to file on behalf of over 400 colleagues, charged that they were segregated to assignments on the U.S.-Mexican border and Puerto Rico, routinely passed over for promotions, denied bonuses payable to bilingual agents, and harassed when they lodged internal complaints. A similar suit, filed by black Secret Service agents in 2000, is still pending.

GETTING HIRED

Each of the Treasury Department's 14 offices recruits separately, including the Legal Division. The Legal Division offers an Honors Program for recent law school graduates and judicial clerks. The Honors Program lasts for two years, and Honors attorneys have worked on several projects, including seizing terrorist funds and negotiating trade agreements. In fact, an Honors attorney can expect exposure to almost all Treasury functions except taxes; the Internal Revenue Service recruits tax attorneys separately. Treasury also hires unpaid interns as Honors Summer Clerkships.

Drug Enforcement Administration

2401 Jefferson Davis Highway
Alexandria, VA 22301
Phone: (202) 307-1000
www.dea.gov

LOCATIONS

Alexandria, VA (HQ)
Field Division Offices in:
Atlanta, GA
Boston, MA
Chicago, IL
Dallas, TX
Denver, CO
Detroit, MI
El Paso, TX
Houston, TX
Los Angeles, CA
Miami, FL
Newark, NJ
New Orleans, LA
New York, NY
Philadelphia, PA
Phoenix, AZ
San Diego, CA
San Francisco, CA
Seattle, WA
St. Louis, MO
Washington, DC
78 foreign offices in 56 countries

THE STATS

No. of employees: 9,600
Acting Administrator: John B. Brown III

EMPLOYMENT CONTACT

http://www.dea.gov/resources/
job_applicants.html

THE SCOOP

In 1973, President Richard Nixon reorganized divisions of the Justice and Treasury departments into a single Drug Enforcement Administration (DEA) under the supervision of the Attorney General. The agency enforces federal laws and regulations concerning controlled substances, and investigates persons and organizations with alleged involvement "in the growing, manufacture, or distribution of controlled substances appearing in or destined for illicit traffic in the United States," delivering those against whom sufficient evidence can be gathered to the U.S. Attorney for prosecution. After the retirement in January 2003 of President Bush's first DEA administrator, former Arkansas congressman Asa Hutchinson, veteran DEA agent and administrator John B. Brown III took over as acting administrator. Brown's tenure with the DEA dates back over thirty years to a stint in its predecessor group, the Bureau of Narcotics and Dangerous Drugs; he has also served as the head of the Dallas field office and the El Paso Intelligence Center, where 15 government agencies collaborate to share information and analysis of drug trafficking operations.

International men of mystery

The DEA has made headway in busting up several international smuggling rings. In June 2002, the DEA secured an indictment against Villanueva Madrid, the former governor of the Mexican state of Quintana Roo, for his role in abetting the Southeast Cartel's shipments of hundreds of tons of cocaine into the United States. The agency also managed an indictment against Consuelo Marquez, a former Lehman Brothers account representative who had helped Madrid set up offshore accounts to launder the $30 million he received from the cartel for allowing them to temporarily store the drugs in his state, in some cases on government property.

In July 2002, Saudi Arabian Prince Nayef Bin Sultan Bin Fawwaz Al-Shaalan was one of four persons named in an indictment on charges of conspiracy to possess with intent to distribute cocaine. A two-year investigation revealed that Al-Shaalan and his accomplices had negotiated with Colombian drug dealers in a number of locations, including Miami, to use his status of diplomatic immunity to transport two tons of cocaine from Venezuela to France in his private jet.

Operation Webslinger

In September 2002, the DEA made a joint announcement with Attorney General John Ashcroft on a major interagency effort it had coordinated with members of the U.S. Postal Inspection Service, U.S. Customs Service, Internal Revenue Service, Federal Bureau of Investigation, the Royal Canadian Mounted Police and the Ontario Police Department. "Operation Webslinger" was the government's largest investigation into the distribution of GHB (an incapacitating depressant often used in sexual assaults) and its derivatives, as well as its largest investigation into online drug trafficking. Targeting both the distributors and the purchasers, the task force arrested 115 people in 84 cities throughout the United States and Canada.

GETTING HIRED

The DEA's web site, www.dea.gov, provides extensive information about certain open positions, including special agents (law enforcement experience is necessary and a law degree won't win you any points). Other positions, including attorney positions, are filled through the federal Office of Personnel Management. A link is available in the DEA career section.

Attorney positions are filled through the federal Office of Personnel Management.

Environmental Protection Agency

1200 Pennsylvania Avenue, NW
Washington, DC 20004
Phone: (202) 260-2090
www.epa.gov

LOCATIONS

Washington, DC (HQ)
Atlanta, GA
Boston, MA
Chicago, IL
Dallas, TX
Denver, CO
Kansas City, KS
Philadelphia, PA
San Francisco, CA
Seattle, WA

THE STATS

No. of other employees: 18,000
Administrator: Christie Whitman
General Counsel: Robert E. Fabricant

EMPLOYMENT CONTACT

http://www.epa.gov/epahome/jobs.htm

THE SCOOP

Trees, water, plants and furry animals

The Environmental Protection Agency (EPA) opened for business in December 1970, the result of a consolidation and reorganization of programs from several departments under one roof at the suggestions of President Richard Nixon. The EPA manages environmental projects (naturally), including programs to prevent and clean up pollution and enforces other environmental laws. The EPA was originally led by former Assistant Attorney General William Doyle Ruckelshaus; it spent much of its first year dealing with the nation's air pollution crisis. By the end of 1972, however, new legislation such as the Federal Environmental Pesticide Control Act and the Ocean Dumping Act enabled the EPA to diversify its mission. Christie Whitman was sworn in as administrator of the EPA in January 2001, a George W. Bush appointee. Before taking over the EPA, Whitman was governor of New Jersey.

Spat with the boss

The EPA was in the news in February 2002 when senior administrator Eric Schaeffer abruptly resigned, stating that the energy industry's influence over the Bush administration had put the agency in the position of "fighting a White House that seems determined to weaken the rules we are trying to enforce." His main grievance stemmed from the government's extended reconsideration of the "New Source Review" provision of the 1990 Clean Air Act, which required older power companies whose high emission levels had been grandfathered to cut back emissions after any large-scale improvements. Several companies charged with violations of this law claimed they had only repaired their systems, not upgraded them, and were waiting out EPA negotiators in the belief the White House would eventually support their interpretation. A spokesman for the president called Schaeffer's allegation "ridiculous" and "unsubstantiated."

Money for clean-ups

In March 2002, Texaco coughed up $850,000 to resolve a federal lawsuit pertaining to approximately 88 oil spills at facilities on Utah's Navajo reservation, some of which they hadn't even notified the EPA about. In addition to a $370,000 penalty, the oil company agreed to fund two environmental projects for the Navajo Nation, including construction of a new water system. In May 2002, the EPA reached an agreement with Exxon Mobil regarding the clean up of the Santa Clara River in California. The company will pay public agencies $4.7 million to reimburse public agencies cleaning up crude oil spilled from a Mobil pipeline in 1991.

The EPA also monitors gas stations to make sure they're properly storing and handling gasoline. In the summer of 2002, the agency reached settlements with Louisiana's Central Oil and Supply Corp. for failing to equip underground tanks and pipes at six stations with proper corrosion protection and leak detectors and with Rhode Island-based Cumberland Farms for using substandard vapor recovery equipment, which helps reduce smog levels, at outlets throughout New England and in New Jersey and Pennsylvania.

GETTING HIRED

Unlike most of the EPA's employees, who go through standard civil service hiring procedures, the agency's attorneys and law clerks are hired directly through 15 human resources offices nationwide. The minimum education requirement for an attorney is a LLB or JD degree and membership in a state bar. Successful applicants for a clerkship receive a 14-month appointment pending admission to the bar.

The EPA's attorneys and law clerks are hired directly through 15 human resources offices nationwide.

Federal Aviation Administration

800 Independence Avenue SW
Washington, DC 20591
Phone: (202) 366-4000
www.faa.gov

LOCATIONS

Washington, DC (HQ)
Anchorage, AK
Atlantic City, NJ
Burlington, MA
College Park, GA
Des Plaines, IL
Ft. Worth, TX
Jamaica, NY
Kansas City, KS
Lawndale, CA
Oklahoma City, OK
Renton, WA

MAJOR DEPARTMENTS & PRACTICES

Aircraft Accident Litigation
Airports and Environmental Law
Contracts and Procurement Law
Industry Regulation
International Aviation Law
Personnel and Labor Law

THE STATS

No. of employees: 44,000+
Administrator: Marion C. Blakey

EMPLOYMENT CONTACT

http://www1.faa.gov/ahr/career/career.htm
http://jobs.faa.gov

THE SCOOP

The wild blue yonder

The Federal Aviation Administration (FAA) was originally an "Agency" when it was founded in 1958; it picked up its current moniker nine years later when it was incorporated into the newly formed Department of Transportation. Its primary responsibility is to maintain the safety of the nation's civil aviation through enforcing regulations concerning the manufacture, operation and maintenance of aircraft, maintaining control of the nation's air traffic and certifying the nation's pilots and airports. As part of the response to September 11, the federal government assumed direct responsibility for airport security in November 2001, and the FAA's Civil Aviation Security branch was incorporated into the newly formed Transportation Security Administration. The administration still plays a role in airport security, however, as in its October 2002 development of new rules governing acceptable forms of photo ID for pilots in flight, and requirements for presenting identification on demand.

Any construction or expansion at airports must receive FAA approval before proceeding, and legal battles have become a common delaying tactic for those seeking to prevent projects from moving forward. The Cleveland suburb of Olmsted Falls sued the FAA, the EPA and other agencies, as well as the mayor of Cleveland and the governor of Ohio, over a half-mile extension to one of the runways at Hopkins International Airport, citing a destructive impact on local wetlands and the displacement of over 200 households in the vicinity. A nonprofit group in Piedmont, NC, challenged the FAA's approval of a $300 million FedEx cargo sorting center to be built at Triad International Airport, claiming that their environmental impact review of the proposal was severely flawed. The complainants were especially concerned about the possible noise pollution caused by 126 daily flights between the hours of 10 p.m. and 7 a.m.

Both the Sierra Club and the California attorney general sued the FAA over its original assessment of expansion plans for an airport at the Mammoth Lakes ski resort, which determined that a full environmental impact statement would not be necessary. Critics charged that the increased air traffic and tourism would create a need for other facilities such as hotels, jeopardizing the habitat of several protected species, including the bighorn sheep and the bald eagle.

Placing blame for a tragedy

Florida-based Cirrus Aviation filed a lawsuit against the FAA in February 2002, blaming confused air traffic controllers for a plane crash at Sarasota-Bradenton International Airport that killed flight instructor Lori Bahrenburg and three other people. A National Transportation Safety Board report on the March 2000 crash determined that controllers had put moved a small plane onto a runway and directly into the path of Bahrenburg's Cessna, which had just started to take off. Cirrus sought $103,100 in damages for lost revenue and increased insurance premiums stemming from the crash; Bahrenburg's parents had previously filed their own multimillion-dollar suit against the administration.

GETTING HIRED

You can find information about FAA job openings at the administration's web site, www.faa.gov, along with downloadable versions of all necessary application forms. The web site also includes benefits and salary information.

Any construction or expansion at airports must receive FAA approval, and legal battles have become a common delaying tactic.

Federal Bureau of Investigation

J. Edgar Hoover Building
935 Pennsylvania Avenue, NW
Washington, DC 20535
Phone: (202) 324-3000
www.fbi.gov

LOCATIONS

Washington, DC

MAJOR DEPARTMENTS & PRACTICES

Administrative and Technology Law
Legal Advice and Training
Litigation
National Security Law

THE STATS

No. of attorneys: 60
No. of other employees: 27,800
Director: Robert S. Mueller III
General Counsel: Kenneth L. Wainstein

EMPLOYMENT CONTACT

http://www.fbi.gov/employment/employ.htm

THE SCOOP

G-men

In 1908, Attorney General Charles Bonaparte established a small corps of special agents within the Department of Justice, rather than continue to rely on private detectives or Secret Service agents for investigative tasks. The group was formally named the Bureau of Investigation a year later by Bonaparte's successor, George Wickersham. J. Edgar Hoover, often misremembered as the bureau's first director, was actually the fifth person to head the agency, taking office in 1924 as part of the government's reshuffling after the death of President Warren G. Harding. It was Hoover who got the "Federal" added on to the bureau's name, a little more than a decade into his 48-year tenure. The first team of agents had very few actual federal crimes to investigate, but the department's mandate expanded over the decades to include fighting violent crimes, sedition, civil rights violations, and organized crime.

Former U.S. Attorney Robert S. Mueller became director just one week before the September 11 terrorist attacks, and though his original priority had been to revamp the FBI's information technology and records management in the aftermath of the scandals surrounding their investigation of the Oklahoma City bombing, he soon found himself overseeing a bureau with a completely new mission, now centered on preventing future attacks, countering other foreign intelligence actions within American borders, and investigating Internet-based and other technology-related crimes.

GETTING HIRED

The FBI has its own jobs web site, www.fbijobs.com, with downloadable Special Agent (SA) application forms and information about other agency positions. The bureau only processes SA applications from candidates who possess critical skills (a listing of which is available on the web site), and does not consider legal expertise a critical need at this time. The bureau does, however, recruit attorneys for support positions. It also takes part in career fairs nationwide on an ongoing basis. Check the site for an upcoming appearance in your area.

If you pass the initial stages of the application process, expect your background check to take anywhere from one to four months. The bureau checks fingerprints, police and employment records. Drug use isn't an automatic disqualification, though those who have used marijuana more than 15 times or within three years of applying are ineligible, as are those who have used other illegal drugs more than five times or within 10 years of their FBI application. Membership in a communist, fascist or terrorist organization will also take you out of the running. Lying on your application, never a good idea, is criminal to the FBI, and is punishable by fines and jail time.

The FBI takes part in career fairs on an ongoing basis. Check fbijobs.com for upcoming appearances.

Federal Communications Commission

445 12th Street, SW
Washington, DC 20554
Phone: (888) 225-5322
www.fcc.gov

LOCATIONS

Washington, DC

MAJOR DEPARTMENTS & PRACTICES

Administrative Law
Litigation
Transaction Team

THE STATS

No. of attorneys: 73
No. of other employees: 1,975
Chairman: Michael K. Powell
General Counsel: Jane E. Mago

UPPERS

- Comfortable lifestyle and hours
- Friendly co-workers

DOWNERS

- Bureaucratic

EMPLOYMENT CONTACT

Job Information Line: (202) 418-0101
http://www.fcc.gov/jobs/

THE SCOOP

Radio heads

The Communications Act of 1934 established a Federal Communications Commission to regulate broadcast and wire communications within the United States and its territories. The commission originally focused on three areas – radio, telegraph, and telephony – but has expanded in response to nearly seven decades of technological advance to include oversight of broadcast and cable television as well as satellite communications.

The FCC's current chairman is Michael Powell, son of Secretary of State Colin Powell. President Bill Clinton first appointed Michael Powell an FCC commissioner in 1997; President George W. Bush bumped Powell up to chairman in 2001. Powell is a graduate of the Georgetown University Law Center and served as chief of staff in the Antitrust Division of the Department of Justice before joining the FCC.

License to sue

The commission's Wireless Communications Bureau is responsible for licensing frequencies on the radio spectrum for use by cellular telephone service providers. In 1996 NextWave won 216 licenses at auction, bidding $4.7 billion. After the company went bankrupt, the FCC took the licenses back and awarded them to other parties for $16 billion. NextWave sued, arguing that the licenses were assets protected under bankruptcy law, and recovered their licenses in 2001, then tentatively agreed to hand them over to the FCC in exchange for $6 billion. When approval for the settlement stalled in Congress, sending everyone back to the negotiating table, one of the new bidders, Verizon Wireless, asked the FCC to return its $1.7 billion deposit, then launched a federal lawsuit to retrieve its money. Meanwhile, the Supreme Court agreed to review the 2001 decision, hearing arguments in early October 2002, but did not appear to hold sympathy for the agency's position that their regulatory authority trumped NextWave's rights under bankruptcy law.

A May 2002 Supreme Court ruling vindicated the guidelines established by the FCC for what the regional Bell networks can charge local phone service competitors for access to their networks. Although Verizon, BellSouth, Qwest and SBC had argued that the FCC's pricing regulations offered them too thin a return on investment in network infrastructure, the justices upheld a 1999 decision that confirmed the commission's authority to set pricing rules as established by the Telecommunications Act. But a three-judge panel from the DC Circuit Court of Appeals vacated a similar policy in United States Telecom Association v. FCC, a case involving sharing of DSL lines. That case is expected to go to the Supreme Court for further review.

The DC Circuit Court also attacked long-standing FCC regulations on media ownership, such as the "eight-voices rule," which prohibits any company from owning more than one television station in a market with fewer than seven other independently owned stations. The rule had been challenged by Sinclair Broadcast Group, which seeks to acquire second stations in six American cities. In a separate lawsuit brought by Fox Television Stations, the court eliminated a regulation banning media companies from owning cable systems and local TV stations in the same market, and ordered the commission to reevaluate a policy preventing television networks from owning local stations in more than 35 percent of the U.S. market. (Fox's acquisition of the Chris-Craft Corporation had already boosted its ownership levels to 40 percent.) These and other decisions prompted the FCC to initiate a comprehensive review of its policies in the summer of 2002, and in September they issued a Notice of Proposed Rule Making (NPRM) inviting public comment on their preliminary findings.

Watch your mouth

Spoken-word artist Sarah Jones sued the FCC in January 2002 over the labeling of "Your Revolution," which quotes lyrics from several hip-hop songs in order to attack their misogyny, as indecent, on the basis of what they called the work's "unmistakable patently offensive sexual references." Jones claimed their evaluation, which prohibits radio stations from playing the song until after 10 p.m., was a violation of her right to free speech. The case was dismissed on procedural grounds, but Jones, represented by prominent media law firm Frankfurt Garbus Kurnit Klein & Selz, promptly filed with the 2nd Circuit Court of Appeals to have the commission's ruling reversed.

Junk fax

In August 2002, the FCC determined that Fax.com had violated the Telephone Consumer Protection Act by sending unsolicited advertisements to fax machines on at least 489 separate occasions. The commission charged the maximum fine of $11,000 on each incident, making the "fax broadcaster's" total liability nearly $5.4 million. In its Notice of Apparent Liability, the commission noted Fax.com's persistence in sending out the offending faxes even after they had first been warned of their potential violations and a consistent pattern of intimidation and deception in the company's dealings with angry consumers who wanted to stop receiving the fax spam.

GETTING HIRED

According to attorneys who are already there, the FCC doesn't make particularly active recruiting efforts, but it does publish job vacancy announcements on its web site, www.fcc.gov, and also maintains a job information phone line. Attorneys are hired into the general counsel, enforcement and inspector general divisions. "Interviews were fairly low stress," says one FCC attorney. "The questions were about substantive background, the appeal of government work vs. the private sector." Another insider touts the importance of "personal contacts and internships" in landing a job with the commission.

OUR SURVEY SAYS

"Overall I am pretty happy with my work at the FCC," one source reports, "much happier than when I was at a large firm." Another attorney who recently joined the Consumer and Governmental Affairs Bureau finds his group "very laid back. Supervisors always have time for questions and discussions. I have gotten a tremendous amount of mentoring." The salaries are "much less than I could make at a firm," admits one insider, but "for me, it's about choosing the kind of life I want and being able to enjoy both my work and my life outside of work, and this job offers that balance." The commission typically expects attorneys to put in just 40 hours a week, and when big projects require overtime, an attorney reports, "the extra hours go towards credit for extra time off."

Attorneys at the FCC see a positive commitment to diversity. "Women play key and often dominant roles here, from low to high levels," an inside source declares, and "there are more minorities in high level positions here than I've seen at firms." And, for the most part, they like their offices as much as they like their jobs. "Office space is limited and you have to work in a cubicle until one opens up," says one. "The cubicles are rather large, though, and many have window views. If you want a good salary, less stress and a life, the FCC is a great place to be. Just remember to pack your own lunch."

"Overall I am pretty happy with my work at the FCC. Much happier than when I was at a large firm."

- FCC attorney

Federal Election Commission

999 E Street, NW
Washington, DC 20463
Phone: (202) 694-1100
www.fec.gov

LOCATIONS

Washington, DC

MAJOR DEPARTMENTS & PRACTICES

(OGC)
Public Funding, Ethics, and Special
  Projects
Policy
Enforcement
Litigation

THE STATS

No. of attorneys: 69 (in 2000)
No. of other employees: 362
(FY2002)
Chair: Ellen L. Weintraub
General Counsel: Lawrence Norton

EMPLOYMENT CONTACT

Tracy Bloom
Office of General Counsel
Federal Election Commission
999 E Street, NW
Washington, DC 20463
http://www.fec.gov/jobs.htm

BASE SALARY

1st Year Attorneys: $48,451 (GS-11,
Step 1)
Interns: $32,736 (GS-7, Step 1)

THE SCOOP

Rock the vote

Throughout the 20th century, concern about disproportionate influence of wealthy contributors over the political process led Congress to pass several campaign financing laws, which it consolidated and amplified in the Federal Election Campaign Act of 1971 (FECA). Three years later, fallout from revelations of financial wrongdoing that emerged during the Watergate scandal inspired the formation of a Federal Election Commission (FEC) to enforce FECA's limits and prohibitions on campaign contributions and disburse public funds, as earmarked on citizens' income tax returns, to presidential campaigns. The six-member commission is intentionally bipartisan; no more than three of its members may belong to any one political party, and a majority vote is required on all decisions. David Mason is the current chairman of the FEC. A 1998 Bill Clinton appointee, Mason has worked in the Department of Defense and behind the scenes for several congressmen.

Follow the money

In March 2002, President George W. Bush reluctantly approved the Bipartisan Campaign Reform Act, popularly known as "McCain-Feingold" after its two Senate sponsors, John McCain of Arizona and Russ Feingold of Wisconsin. The law called for a complete ban on unrestricted "soft money" contributions (i.e., donations individuals and organizations can make to political parties as opposed to directly contributing to candidates' campaign funds). Two days after signing the bill, Bush took advantage of a Senate recess to appoint one of its sharpest critics, Republican National Committee counsel Michael Toner, to the FEC. Toner insisted that he would fairly enforce the law, but in June the commission voted, against the advice of its own attorneys, to narrow the restriction so tightly that the only way a candidate for federal office could violate the ban on raising soft money would be to ask for it directly.

This, along with several other decisions easing the restrictions on soft money mandated by the BCRA, led its sponsors in the House of Representatives, Christopher Shays and Marty Meehan, to file a federal lawsuit in October asking the court to force the FEC to craft new regulations that lived up to the requirements Congress had set.

Meanwhile several groups had already begun challenging the law in the federal court system. The National Rifle Association and the Christian Coalition argued in separate lawsuits that the new restrictions violated their constitutional rights to free speech, as did a half dozen teenage activists who challenged a provision in the law banning financial contributions of any kind by minors. Fundraising committees for both the Democratic and Republican parties also filed suit, then grappled with FEC attorneys over how much information concerning their operations they would have to share during the discovery process. The FEC sought full documentation, but agreed with both sides to settle for sworn affidavits backed up by a sampling of internal documents.

A legal spending spree?

In September 2002, the commission's attorneys raised a radical possible interpretation of the new law, suggesting that political parties might be permitted to spend unlimited amounts of money in direct support of their presidential nominees. While political parties are limited in the amount of money they can spend in coordination with the candidate's campaign, especially when the candidate receives public funding, the counsel's proposal suggested that it might be legal for parties to spend unlimited amounts of money on a nominee if they didn't coordinate their spending with the campaign.

GETTING HIRED

The FEC announces job vacancies on its web site, www.fec.gov, where you can also find a PDF version of a pamphlet published by the commission's Office of General Counsel on the opportunities "to work with cases and issues which directly impact the American political process." The office actively seeks third-year law students and experienced attorneys "who have a commitment to public service and an interest in the political process." The FEC hires approximately five summer law clerks every year. Most summers are second-years but first-years are occasionally considered.

Hiring managers at the FEC tell Vault that the agency prefers students with law review and moot court experience who are in the top third of their class. Applicants should include a cover letter, resume, writing sample and transcript when applying to the employment contact listed on the previous page.

"Work with cases and issues which directly impact the American political process."

- FEC web site

Federal Emergency Management Agency

500 C Street, SW
Washington, DC 20472
Phone: (202) 566-1600
www.fema.gov

LOCATIONS

Washington, DC (HQ)
Atlanta, GA
Boston, MA
Bothell, WA
Chicago, IL
Denton, TX
Denver, CO
Kansas City, MO
New York, NY
Oakland, CA
Philadelphia, PA

THE STATS

No. of attorneys: 30
No. of other employees: 2,600
Undersecretary of Emergency Preparedness and Response:
Michael Brown

EMPLOYMENT CONTACT

http://www.fema.gov/career/index.jsp

THE SCOOP

Rescue me

The tradition of federal assistance to American disaster victims extends back as far as 1803, but for over a hundred years it was on an ad hoc basis requiring specific Congressional legislation. In the 1930s, agencies such as the Reconstruction Finance Corporation received broader authority to provide relief, but the decentralized approach created bureaucratic delays, even after the 1974 Disaster Relief Act enabled the president to make "disaster area" declarations. To streamline the process, President Jimmy Carter issued an executive order in 1979 establishing a Federal Emergency Management Agency (FEMA). Its mandate included not only natural disasters such as earthquakes and floods, but also crises involving hazardous substances or terrorist attacks.

After the terrorist attacks of September 11, the Bush administration created a plan for a new Cabinet-level organization, the Department of Homeland Security, which would incorporate a wide variety of preexisting government organizations, including FEMA. As that plan solidified, Joe Allbaugh, the longtime Bush adviser appointed to direct the agency in 2001, announced his retirement. Bush nominated Michael Brown, the agency's deputy director and former general counsel, to take over FEMA under the new job title of Under Secretary of Emergency Preparedness and Response.

In June 2002, the 9th Circuit Court of Appeals reversed an earlier federal court decision requiring the Hawaiian state government to reimburse FEMA for relief funds provided to repair the devastation of 1992's Hurricane Iniki. The agency claimed Hawaii was not entitled to duplicate benefits for damages on which the state had also collected from private insurance companies. Hawaii acknowledged owing some money, but not the $12.1 million FEMA sought. The appeals court, in reviewing the case, determined that Hawaii had acted reasonably in settling quickly with the insurance companies and had not tried to defraud the federal government.

FEMA's National Flood Insurance Program requires participating communities to adopt land use restrictions aimed at reducing the risks of future damages. But their guidelines came under fire from a number of environmental groups, including the Sierra Club, who filed a lawsuit alleging FEMA had encouraged New Mexicans to build along riverbanks that are home to several endangered species. The agency settled with the groups in 2002, agreeing to reassess its requirements for communities in the Rio

Grande flood plains to ensure that they comply with the Endangered Species Act.

GETTING HIRED

The FEMA web site, www.fema.gov, lists all available positions at the administration's national headquarters and regional offices. Be sure to read all application instructions carefully: FEMA has made changes in its mail handling system in response to the anthrax scare in late 2001, and any non-compliance with application requirements will result in being immediately dropped from consideration for employment.

Any non-compliance with application requirements at FEMA will result in being immediately dropped from consideration for employment.

Federal Reserve Board

2001 C Street NE
Washington, DC 20002
Phone: (202) 452-3000
www.federalreserve.gov

LOCATIONS

Washington, DC (HQ)
Boston, MA
New York, NY
Philadelphia, PA
Cleveland, OH
Richmond, VA
Atlanta, GA
Chicago, IL
St. Louis, MO
Minneapolis, MN
Kansas City, MO
Dallas, TX
San Francisco, CA

THE STATS

No. of employees: 1,700
Chairman: Alan Greenspan

BASE SALARY

1st year: $76,530

EMPLOYMENT CONTACT

Board of Governors of the Federal
  Reserve System
Recruitment Office, Mail Stop 129
20th and C Streets, NW
Washington, DC 20551

Job Vacancy Line: (800) 448-4894
http://www.federalreserve.gov/careers/
default.cfm

THE SCOOP

America's ATM

Congress created the Federal Reserve Bank (commonly known as the Fed) in 1913 to provide some much needed stability to the American financial system. It has evolved into one of the most powerful influences over the nation's economy, as its seven-member board of governors strives to fulfill its mandate "to promote effectively the goals of maximum employment, stable prices, and moderate long-term interest rates."

The Federal Reserve derives much of its power from its independence. It receives no funding from the government; in fact, it ends up supplying the Treasury Department with billions of dollars each year. The Fed's governors are each appointed to a single fourteen-year term that could, in theory, span the administration of as many as four presidents. (However, if a board member is chosen to fill out the remaining portion of an unexpired term, he may serve again for a full term, as in the case of Fed Chairman Alan Greenspan, who first joined the Board in 1987 and was reappointed in 1992.)

The Board doesn't just set America's monetary policy. It also has regulatory authority over banks that participate in the Reserve system. So when Citigroup announced its intention to buyout Golden State Bancorp in 2002, the Fed launched a full review into the financial service company's activities, particularly the subprime lending practices of its CitiFinancial Credit division. Although many analysts remained confident that the merger would be approved, the inquiry came at a difficult time for Citigroup, which had to settle a $215 million Federal Trade Commission lawsuit over CitiFinancial's lending practices and became involved in criminal investigations by the New York state attorney general's office into Citigroup's brokerage division, Salomon Smith Barney, and a Manhattan district attorney's inquiry into the bank's handling of Enron's finances.

GETTING HIRED

The Fed is looking for attorneys with excellent grades and coursework or extracurricular activities that indicate a strong interest in the Board's responsibilities. Law review also helps. Attorneys are hired for the legal division (to interpret and advise on legislation, policy and other Fed activities), banking supervision and regulation and consumer and community affairs (to deal with consumer credit regulations). You can find listings for all open attorney positions on the Fed's web site, www.federalreserve.gov.

The Board has regulatory authority over banks that participate in the Reserve system.

Federal Trade Commission

600 Pennsylvania Avenue, NW
Washington, DC 20580
Phone: (202) 326-2222
www.ftc.gov

LOCATIONS

Washington, DC (HQ)
Atlanta, GA
Chicago, IL
Cleveland, OH
Dallas, TX
Los Angeles, CA
New York, NY
San Francisco, CA
Seattle, WA

THE STATS

No. of attorneys: 640
No. of other employees: 550
Chairman: Timothy J. Muris
General Counsel: William E.
Kovacic

BASE SALARY

Washington, DC (2003)
1st year: $57,495

EMPLOYMENT CONTACT

Human Resources Management Office
Attn: Attorney Recruitment Office
Federal Trade Commission
600 Pennsylvania Avenue, NW
Washington, DC 20580
E-mail: HRMO@ftc.gov

THE SCOOP

The consumer's best friend

The Federal Trade Commission (FTC) has the authority to enforce and administrate 46 federal antitrust and consumer protection laws. The laws cover a range of trade issues, from corporate mergers and the threat of commercial monopolies to the accurate labeling of wool products and "dolphin safe" tuna to restrictions on telemarketing calls. Their ultimate intent is to make the market work to the best advantages of the consumer by preventing vendors from engaging in anticompetitive, deceptive or unfair practices.

In April 2002, for example, the FTC obtained a preliminary injunction from the U.S. District Court for the District of Columbia blocking the acquisition of Anchor Hocking Co., a division of Newell Rubbermaid, by Libbey, the nation's largest vendor of food service glassware. Because Anchor was the nation's third-largest maker and seller of soda-lime glassware, which Libbey also produces, the FTC determined the proposed merger would create an unlawful soda-lime glassware monopoly. On the basis of this injunction, Libbey abandoned the buyout plan in June; two months later, it reached an agreement to formally notify the commission before making any subsequent attempts to acquire any ownership stake in Anchor or its assets in the following decade; the order also requires Newell to notify the commission of its intention to sell Anchor to any other purchaser.

The FTC recently went after two pharmaceutical manufacturers, Schering-Plough and Upsher-Smith Laboratories, accusing them of colluding to keep prescription drug prices high by delaying the commercial availability of a generic version of Schering's potassium chloride supplement K-Dur 20. An administrative law judge ruled in June 2002 that the FTC had failed to meet its burden of proof in support of the allegations and dismissed the charges. The following month, the commission issued proposed legislative changes aimed at ensuring consumers will have generic drugs made available to them in a more timely fashion.

She should have seen it coming

Even the clairvoyant need fear the FTC. The commission filed a complaint in February 2002 against two Florida companies, Access Resource Services and Psychic Readers Network, for deceptive advertising, billing and collecting practices related to their joint management of the Miss Cleo franchise. Consumers complained that televisions ads featuring the all-knowing Miss Cleo falsely promised "free" psychic readings and that the company lied to customers about the fees they were racking up, then threatened them with overinflated service charges. The two companies settled with the FTC in November, closing up shop and wiping out $500 million in customer charges. The settlement was the largest in FTC history.

The New York State Bar Association and American Bar Association sued the FTC in September 2002 over the agency's interpretation of the Gramm-Leach-Bliley Act. The 1999 law, also known as the Financial Services Modernization Act, set up rules for how banks and other financial institutions could use customer information and required disclosure of banks' privacy policies. The FTC has interpreted the law's wording as applicable to lawyers, while the bar associations have argued that the ethical codes governing lawyers (including attorney-client privilege) are sufficient to protect clients' rights. The suit is pending, as is legislation in Congress that would specifically exempt law firms from the Gramm-Leach-Bliley Act.

Protecting your inbox

The agency has taken on the responsibility of dealing with spam. The FTC receives 50,000 consumer complaints about unsolicited e-mail advertising every day, but federal law limits it to prosecuting only those online advertisers who make deceptive claims. They did that with a vengeance, however, teaming up with law enforcement officials in several states, and across the border in Canada, to file numerous complaints of Internet fraud. In April 2002, the FTC-led Northwest Netforce announced 63 separation actions against spammers; a Midwestern task force brought 19 additional cases the following July.

GETTING HIRED

According to its web site, www.ftc.gov, the Federal Trade Commission recruits strongly among "talented and dedicated law students with an exceptional level of commitment to the public interest to enforcing antitrust and consumer protection laws as mandated by Congress." Recent law school graduates begin a 14-month law clerk's position pending their admission to a state bar. Summer internships are also available to students about to start their last year of law school or recent graduates who will begin judicial clerkships in the fall.

General Accounting Office

441 G Street, NW
Washington, DC 20548
Phone: (202) 512-6000
www.gao.gov

LOCATIONS

Washington, DC (HQ)
Atlanta, GA
Boston, MA
Chicago, IL
Dallas, TX
Dayton, OH
Denver, CO
Huntsville, AL
Los Angeles, CA
Norfolk, VA
San Francisco, CA
Seattle, WA

THE STATS

No. of attorneys: 30 +
No. of other employees: 3,200
Comptroller General: David M. Walker
General Counsel: Anthony Gamboa

EMPLOYMENT CONTACT

https://jobs.quickhire.com/scripts/gao.exe

THE SCOOP

Department of bean counting

Faced with a growing national debt after the end of the World War I, Congress passed the Budget and Accounting Act of 1921 requiring the president to draft an annual federal budget and establishing a General Accounting Office (GAO) to assume auditing, accounting and claims functions that had until that point been handled through the Treasury Department. In over 80 years of independent service to Congress, it has undertaken numerous audits of other government agencies, verifying that they meet their financial and performance objectives to provide top-quality service to the American public. The GAO also functions as an investigative agency, considering allegations of illegal or improper activities in other divisions of the government.

The GAO is headed by the Comptroller General, who is appointed to a 15-year term that enables him to fulfill his duties without the pressures of partisan politics. The current Comptroller General, David Walker, was appointed to the office by President Clinton in 1998, and had previously served as an assistant secretary in the Department of Labor during the Reagan Administration. Between his stints of government service, he was a partner at Arthur Andersen and the global managing director of their human capital services practice.

A subpoena for the VP

A investigation into Vice President Dick Cheney's energy task force set a new precedent in February 2002 when Comptroller General Walker filed a lawsuit against Cheney in an attempt to force him to provide the GAO with documents concerning his role in the committee's proceedings. The office's inquiry focused on how the vice president had selected outside advisers to the National Energy Policy Development Group and where the money to host the task force's meetings came from. In his refusal to hand over the documents, Cheney cited executive privilege, and the Justice Department argued on his behalf that the group's activities were beyond the GAO's purview. Lawyers for the office countered that its authority to audit government spending and operations extends to the executive branch, but a federal judge rejected their reasoning in December, dismissing the lawsuit on the grounds that, since no congressional committee had authorized the office to file its suit or subpoenaed the records for its own investigation, the comptroller general could not demonstrate that he had been injured by Cheney's refusal.

Senator Patrick Leahy (a Vermont Democrat), the chairman of the Senate Judiciary Committee, asked the GAO in March 2002 to investigate the possibility that former independent counsel Robert Ray had broken federal law by planning his brief campaign for a U.S. Senate seat in New Jersey while still employed as a federal prosecutor. This request came soon after Leahy had written to the GAO concerning a memo from Attorney General John Ashcroft advising federal agencies that they could withhold documents from Freedom of Information Act (FOI) requests with the Justice Department's full support. Leahy asked the GAO to determine whether an increase in withholding of government documents had occurred and if the memo had caused a backlog of FOIA requests or lawsuits against federal agencies for withholding records.

The GAO also reviews disputes involving bids for government contracts. In May 2002, the owners of the Bath Iron Works shipyard protested the awarding of a $2.9 billion Navy project for a new high-tech vessel, a stealth destroyer called the DD-X, to rival shipbuilders Northrop Grumman. General Dynamics argued that the Navy based their decision on a separate contract with Northrop Grumman's partner, Raytheon, which was not supposed to influence the selection of the DD-X design team. The GAO's review of the bidding process determined three months later, in a somewhat ambiguous statement from a staff attorney, that "the Navy hadn't violated procurement law in any way that hurt Bath Iron Works," leaving open the question of whether the Navy had violated procurement law in other ways.

GETTING HIRED

The GAO recruits attorneys into its Office of General Counsel. The office assists GAO analysts with their work and responds to legal challenges and congressional requests. Other attorneys work with the GAO's investigative unit. Entry-level attorneys rotate through several departments before being assigned to a permanent appointment. The GAO recruits summer associates that work in one or two departments. Use the office's web site, www.gao.gov, to access GAO Careers, a computerized application processing system that allows you to apply for current openings or preregister for jobs that aren't currently available.

Entry-level attorneys rotate through several departments before being assigned to a permanent appointment.

General Services Administration

1800 F Street, NW
Washington, DC 20405
Phone: (202) 501-0800
www.gsa.gov

LOCATIONS

Washington, DC (HQ)
Boston, MA
New York, NY
Philadelphia, PA
Atlanta, GA
Chicago, IL
Kansas City, MO
Fort Worth, TX
Denver, CO
San Francisco, CA
Auburn, WA

THE STATS

No. of employees: 14,000
Adminstrator: Stephen A. Perry
General Counsel: Raymond J. McKenna

EMPLOYMENT CONTACT

Jeanette Artis
Office of General Counsel
1800 F Street NW
Washington, DC 20405
Phone: (202) 501-0481

THE SCOOP

The government's office manager

When Harry Truman asked former president Herbert Hoover to head a commission to find ways to enable the government to perform its administrative functions more efficiently, he came up with nearly 300 separate recommendations. One of them was to consolidate four agencies with responsibility for federal supplies into a single, streamlined organization, and the Federal Property and Administrative Services Act of 1949 enacted his proposal through the creation of the General Services Administration (GSA). The GSA maintains the physical infrastructure of the rest of the federal government: finding, procuring and managing facilities, supplying agencies with furniture, technology and other equipment, installing telecommunications systems, even running transportation services and child care centers at some government offices. It also serves as the managing partner on several components of the White House's "E-government" strategy, which enables citizens and businesses to obtain a number of services from the government online.

Surplus government land

As part of its handling of the federal government's real estate concerns, the General Services Administration runs an Office of Property Disposal to sell land and buildings which the government no longer needs. After months of negotiation with the GSA, supervisors in Fairfax County, Va., voted unanimously in April 2002 to purchase the 2,323-acre site of the defunct Lorton federal prison complex. The county agreed to pay $4.23 million for the property, which features many rolling hills and open spaces. Nearly two-thirds of the land will be used for parks and recreational facilities, but 136 of the 300 buildings on the property are designated as historically significant and the county will have to cooperate with the federal government in determining their use.

The GSA's efforts to get rid of a former army ammunition plant in Kansas, however, continued to suffer from legal complications. Although the agency had considered a bid from Oz Entertainment, which planned to build a Wizard of Oz theme park on the site, the United Tribe of Shawnee Indians stepped forward in 1999, claiming their right to the land. The tribe's lawsuit was dismissed by the Kansas U.S. District Court on the grounds that the Shawnee were not recognized as a legitimate tribe because of an 1869 pact incorporating its members into the Cherokee Nation. The 10th Circuit Court of Appeals upheld the dismissal, but in the meantime, a group of Kansans against the theme park filed their own lawsuit accusing the GSA of violating the National Historic Preservation Act and the National Environmental Policy Act. Oz Entertainment ditched its plans, leaving the GSA to find a new buyer for the site.

As the managers for federal property, the GSA issues permits to groups wishing to hold demonstrations outside federal office buildings. The American Civil Liberties Union (ACLU) filed suit against the agency in 2001, demanding that it rescind a policy against issuing permits for simultaneous demonstrations in downtown Chicago's Federal Plaza. The ACLU charged that this policy prohibited groups from holding counter-demonstrations against groups with opposing viewpoints. The GSA conceded the issue in an October 2002 settlement, approved by a U.S. District Court judge in the Dirksen Federal Building, right across the street.

GETTING HIRED

The GSA's web site, www.gsa.gov, has basic information about available jobs. Attorneys can be hired into the Office of the Inspector General. Since those are law enforcement positions, you'll have to take a complete physical and a drug test as well as submit to a background check.

Attorneys can be hired into the Office of the Inspector General. Since those are law enforcement positions, you'll have to take a complete physical and a drug test as well as submit to a background check.

Human Rights Watch

350 Fifth Avenue, 34th floor
New York, NY 10118
Phone: (212) 290-4700
www.hrw.org

LOCATIONS

New York, NY (HQ)
Washington DC
Los Angeles, CA
San Francisco, CA
London
Brussels
Moscow

MAJOR DEPARTMENTS & PRACTICES

Arms
Children's Rights
HIV/AIDS
International Justice
Prisons
Refugees
Religious Freedom
Women's Rights

THE STATS

No. of attorneys: 3
No. of other employees: 180
Executive Director: Kenneth Roth
General Counsel: Dinah PoKempner

UPPERS

- Empowering work on important human rights issues
- Informal, friendly office

DOWNERS

- Low pay
- Mundane administrative work

EMPLOYMENT CONTACT

Maria Pignataro Nielsen
Director, Human Resources
350 Fifth Avenue
34th Floor
New York, NY 10118-3299
http://www.hrw.org/jobs/

THE SCOOP

Keeping tabs on the evil empire

Human Rights Watch (HRW) started in 1978 as Helsinki Watch, and focused exclusively on assisting activist groups in Soviet bloc countries who, acting upon the Helsinki Accords in which 35 European nations affirmed "the right of the individual to know and act upon his rights," monitored their governments and documented human rights violations. Americas Watch and Asia Watch followed in 1981 and 1985, respectively, and in 1988 the three committees combined with the Prison Project to form HRW. (Other Watch committees, concentrating on Africa and the Middle East, launched their efforts within a year of the merger.)

In the quarter century since its founding, HRW has become the largest U.S.-based human rights organization, with over 180 professionals and countless volunteers. Human Rights Watch addresses a number of issues, from censorship and discrimination to military conduct during wartime. They routinely publish the results of their investigations, and try to persuade governments to stop violating citizens' rights. When that doesn't work, HRW turns to powerful institutions such as the United Nations and the U.S. government to put further pressure on the leaders of abusive regimes.

Eye on America

Human Rights Watch spent a great deal of time in 2002 monitoring the activities of the Bush administration, including the government's efforts to exempt its military and civilian personnel from the jurisdiction of the International Criminal Court. The organization also closely scrutinized the government's activities following the terrorist attacks of September 11, frequently highlighting the civil rights violations in proposed homeland security legislation. In August 2002, they released a 95-page report, "Presumption of Guilt: Human Rights Abuses of Post-September 11 Detainees," which drew upon interviews with some of the 1,200 immigrants held by the Justice Department. The investigators determined that "the U.S. government has held some detainees for prolonged periods without charges; impeded their access to counsel; subjected them to coercive interrogations; and overridden judicial orders to release them on bond during immigration proceedings." The group also collaborated with the American Civil Liberties Union and other organizations in one of the many suits against the government aimed at forcing the disclosure of the names of those detainees.

U.S. District Judge Gladys Kessler ordered the government to release the names in August, but then granted a delay while the Justice Department worked on its appeal.

As President Bush mulled over the possibility of military intervention in Iraq, Human Rights Watch argued for another approach: indicting Saddam Hussein in international court for his atrocities, especially the 1988 genocidal campaign against Iraqi Kurds. The U.S. government had previously shown some interest in this approach; two Defense Department lawyers even spoke with an HRW researcher while preparing their own report on Hussein's activities. But the Bush administration, growing skeptical towards war crimes tribunals, classified its findings and shelved the report for future use.

Children's rights in Burma

In October 2002, HRW published "My Gun Was as Tall as Me," a report on forced military inscription in the Union of Myanmar (formerly known as Burma) of children as young as 11, who were then brutally treated and forced into combat against armed rebels. "All of us told the soldiers we didn't want to join the army and some said they were students, and the soldiers punched us," one 12-year-old "recruit" testified, "They asked me, 'Do you want to join the army? I refused and they punched me. Then they asked again, 'Do you want to join the army?' I refused again and they punched me again." The government was quick to denounce the report as an attempt to shame Myanmar in the international community, insisting that military service was purely voluntary and limited to those over the age of 18.

Richard Dicker, the head of HRW's International Justice Program, monitored the international tribunal prosecuting former Serbian leader Slobodan Milosevic throughout 2002, as it proceeded from evidence of human rights violations during the fighting in Kosovo to earlier war crimes committed in Bosnia-Herzegovina and Croatia. Throughout the 1990s, Human Rights Watch published reports on many of the violations with which Milosevic is charged, including atrocities that took place in Sarajevo and Srebrenica.

Human Rights Watch continues to monitor the former Soviet republics, and has been extremely vocal about the ongoing abuses in Kyrgyzstan and Uzbekistan. They've also kept a close watch on Turkey's application for membership in the European Union, and have prepared documents to inform EU leadership of the advances the Turkish government had made on human rights issues, such as abolishing the death penalty, as well as the continuing practice of torture and suppression of free speech.

GETTING HIRED

The Human Rights Watch web site, www.hrw.org, periodically updates its list of available job openings and keeps any new position on the site for at least a month. The organization also spreads news of vacancies throughout the human rights community, on sites such as www.idealist.org. "I went out on my own and applied for a fellowship and a staff researcher position," one source tells us. "The interview process was very rigorous and included a lot of tough questions and a writing assignment. It was not like a schmoozy law firm interview." Another staffer confirms that "recruitment here usually involves both interviews and written exercises, which is useful since so much writing is involved." Fluency in foreign languages will be a major asset, and international travel can also work in your favor, as will previous experience with nonprofit organizations.

OUR SURVEY SAYS

"Our base salary is extremely low for New York," the HRW staff surveyed all agree. "I feel grossly underpaid," one elaborates, "and would not be able to make monthly loan payments if I had them. Still, I went into this with my eyes open." But the organization benefits package compares favorably to those available throughout the nonprofit sector. In addition to three to four weeks vacation, "we can audit classes at the New School for free and the organization will pay for half of classes at other universities." Everybody says the financials were not their first consideration in accepting a position with the organization. "I may want to do law teaching at some point," one legal researcher explains, "and this seems like good preparation. I also was frustrated with my lack of expertise in issues I cared a lot about."

"Being surrounded by motivated, passionate people is a definite plus," says one Human Rights Watch employee, "along with the trainings and meetings that even low level associates are welcome to sit in on." Another source comments, "It feels more like a law firm than you might expect. Long, narrow corridors with people working behind closed doors, usually very quietly." HRW staffers rated the organization positively on all diversity issues, although one employee confides, "I expected the office culture to be more gay-positive than it is. I haven't experienced any discrimination, and there are openly gay people in leadership positions, but there are a handful of fairly conservative folks here."

As in any office environment, nobody is always happy with the way things are run. "Some directors are very hierarchical, others very stressed out," observes one HRW member. "Others clearly have pet projects and marginalize others." But they all appreciate what one source calls "the privilege of helping to tell the story of people around the world who suffer human rights abuses." Plus, as another employee notes, "I work hard but have total control over my schedule. I can avoid working on weekends for the most part, and I rarely stay past 7:00 p.m."

"Being surrounded by motivated, passionate people is a definite plus."

– HRW attorney

Internal Revenue Service

1111 Constitution Avenue, NW
Washington, DC 20224
Phone: (202) 622-2000
www.irs.gov

THE STATS

No. of attorneys: 1,500
No. of other employees: 99,900
Acting Commissioner: Robert E. Wenzel
Chief Counsel: B. John Williams Jr.

BASE SALARY

1st year: $41,684

EMPLOYMENT CONTACT

Attorney Recruitment Office
Internal Revenue Service
111 Constitution Ave., NW
Washington, DC 20224
http://www.jobs.irs.gov/

THE SCOOP

Tax men

The American government first instituted a national income tax in 1862, to help pay for the Civil War, but it was never popular, and Congress repealed it just a decade later. An attempt was made to resurrect the income tax in 1894, but the Supreme Court struck the tax law down the following year. The 16th Amendment to the U.S. Constitution, ratified in 1913, gave Congress the right to levy and collect income taxes. The Treasury Department created a Bureau of Internal Revenue to collect them. The department's name was changed to the Internal Revenue Service (IRS) in the 1950s to emphasize its taxpayer service aspects over its administration of the tax code.

Charles O. Rossotti, appointed as the 45th Commissioner of Internal Revenue by President Bill Clinton, completed his five-year term in 2002. Until the Bush administration named a formal replacement, Bob Wenzel, an IRS official with nearly forty years of experience at the agency, served as acting commissioner. Rossotti fought hard in the final two years of his term for budget increases to hire additional agents to enforce the tax code against tax cheats, but ran afoul of the Bush administration's preferred emphasis on tax reform.

Hot tips

The IRS's interpretation of laws regarding tip income was upheld by the Supreme Court in September 2002. In the early 1990s, an IRS audit of San Francisco restaurant Fior d'Italia determined the eatery owed $23,000 in unpaid Social Security taxes because it had failed to properly account for its servers' tips. Fior d'Italia challenged the IRS decision, saying the government should penalize the employees who had underreported tips. The Supreme Court ruled that it was the employer's responsibility to keep tabs on its staff's tip income and ordered Fior d'Italia to pay up.

Tax-shelter probes

The IRS undertook a major investigation into tax shelters, pressing several major accounting firms to comply with laws that require tax shelter promoters to register their shelters with the IRS and provide the agency with a list of investors upon demand. In July 2002, shortly after having reached an agreement with PricewaterhouseCoopers, they had the Department of Justice file lawsuits against BDO Seidman and KPMG, who had been stonewalling on the records the agency sought. But the documents filed by U.S. Attorneys included the names of several KPMG clients, including the Republican candidate in the California governor's race, the chairs of Global Crossing and New Line Cinema, and the late Dale Earnhardt. General counsel for both the IRS and the Treasury Department immediately apologized for the disclosure, saying that the documents should have been put under court seal.

Refund suits

When the appeals process fails, some folks believe so strongly they're entitled to a refund they're willing to go to court over disputes that began over a decade ago. Laurence Eustelle Wolff, of Gillette, Wyo., fought a $291,000 bill covering the years 1988-1995, arguing in an April 2002 lawsuit that none of the liens the IRS had issued on his property were legally valid. Later that year, consumer paper products manufacturer Kimberly-Clark claimed they had been overtaxed for over $12 million during a two-year period in the 1980s in which the government denied the company credit for foreign taxes paid through European subsidiaries. Both cases are pending.

GETTING HIRED

The IRS hires attorneys into its Office of Chief Counsel; approximately 45 percent work in Washington, DC, with the rest spread around 50 regional offices. The agency hires 40 law school graduates each year for law clerk positions in the IRS Office of Chief Counsel's Honors Program. The program gives third-year law students and recent graduates an opportunity to begin working for the IRS immediately while preparing to become members of a state bar. Second- and first-year law students can be hired into the agency's summer intern program in Washington and select locations around the U.S. Law students can work on an unpaid "externship" during the academic year. The IRS also hires approximately 60 attorneys with one to three years of tax law experience through a lateral hiring program.

The agency hires 40 law school graduates each year for law clerk positions in the IRS Office of Chief Counsel's Honors Program.

Lawyers Committee for Human Rights

333 Seventh Avenue
13th Floor
New York, NY 10001-5004
Phone: (212) 845 5200
www.lchr.org

LOCATIONS

New York, NY (HQ)
Oakland, CA
Washington, DC

MAJOR DEPARTMENTS & PRACTICES

Human Rights
Political Refugees
Workers' Rights

THE STATS

No. of attorneys: 25
No. of other employees: 65
Executive Director: Michael Posner

EMPLOYMENT CONTACT

Kathy Jones
Director of Human Resources and
 Special Projects
333 Seventh Avenue
13th Floor
New York, NY 10001-5004

http://www.lchr.org/about_us/
about_us.htm

BASE SALARY

$30,000-$50,000, depending on
experience

THE SCOOP

Fighting for rights

The Lawyers Committee for Human Rights (LCHR) was established in 1978 and led for nearly two decades by Jerome Shestack, a litigator and civil rights attorney who also served as the U.S. Ambassador for Human Rights to the United Nations Human Rights Commission during the Carter administration. The LCHR works in the United States and abroad to, as the agency's mission statement declares, "[advance] justice, human dignity and respect for the rule of law."

Shortly before the one-year anniversary of the terrorist attacks on the World Trade Center and Pentagon, LCHR released "A Year of Loss: Reexamining Civil Liberties since September 11." The report extensively cataloged several aspects of the Bush administration's response to the attacks, including restrictions on the public's access to information about governmental proceedings, the erosion of privacy rights by new "counter-terrorist" legislation, and the mistreatment of detainees by the Justice Department (including, in many cases, denial of access to legal counsel). Furthermore, the report noted, "In lowering [its] own human rights standards, the U.S. has moved, though in some cases inadvertently, to lower the standards of human rights around the world."

International justice

Through its Human Rights Defenders' Project, LCHR advocates for human rights activists around the world who are working for reform within their own countries. When governments attempt to retaliate against those reformers, LCHR makes sure that foreign leaders and international media know about it. Shortly after the terrorist attacks of September 11, they launched a special initiative to assist activists in the Middle East, hoping to foster political openness in several countries in the region and expand opportunities for peaceful forms of dissent. When the Egyptian parliament passed legislation in June 2002 that would effectively make it impossible to run a non-governmental organization, LCHR wrote a position paper decrying the proposal as an attempt to suppress political dissent and publicly urged President Bush to press Egypt's leader, Hosni Mubarak, to veto the bill. (Their efforts failed.)

The Lawyers Committee played a strong role in establishing the war crimes tribunals against former leaders in Yugoslavia and Rwanda, and has actively advocated for the establishment of the permanent International Criminal Court (ICC). When the United States government indicated its unwillingness to allow the ICC to judge its activities, and demanded unilateral amnesty, LCHR lobbied other nations to maintain a united front against the Bush administration's stance, and not to sign treaties that would prevent the ICC from prosecuting Americans for acts committed within their borders. They also helped organize petition drives in the United States.

The Lawyers Committee has advocated for workers' rights through both legislative lobbying and by promoting the concept of "corporate responsibility" - holding corporations responsible for their treatment of workers around the world. When a group of Indonesian villagers sued Exxon Mobil within the U.S. court system under the Alien Tort Claims Act for abuses perpetrated by Indonesian security forces hired by the oil company to protect its refineries, for example, LCHR was among the groups who urged the State Department not to advise the judge, as it eventually did, that "adjudication of this lawsuit would in fact risk a potentially serious adverse impact on significant interests of the United States."

The group has fought for the rights of international refugees since its founding. In recent years, changes in U.S. immigration law have made it increasingly difficult for foreigners seeking political asylum, with many refugees being deported almost immediately after they've arrived. Those who don't face "expedited removal" can be subject to mandatory detention for unlimited amounts of time while the government investigates their claims. LCHR is working with members of both houses of Congress to develop a "Refugee Protection Act" that would counteract the worst of those injustices.

GETTING HIRED

The LCHR website, www.lchr.org, has information about current job openings within the organization. The group also offers several internship positions each year. Although the committee does not compensate its interns directly, they are usually eligible for grants from outside organizations (the Lawyers Committee specifically mentions the Everett Foundation, a group that sponsors nonprofit internships) or from their universities.

"To create a secure and humane world by advancing justice, human dignity and respect for the rule of law."

- LCHR mission statement

Lawyers' Committee for Civil Rights Under Law

1401 New York Avenue, NW
Suite 400
Washington, DC 20005
Phone: (202) 662-8600
www.lawyerscomm.org

LOCATIONS

Washington, DC (HQ)

MAJOR DEPARTMENTS & PRACTICES

Education
Employment
Environment Justice
Housing
Lending and Community
　　Development
Voting Rights

THE STATS

No. of attorneys: 10
No. of other employees: 37
Executive Director: Barbara R.
Arnwine
Counsel: Nicholas T. Christakos

THE SCOOP

Heeding JFK's call

In 1963 President John F. Kennedy put out a request to the nation's lawyers, asking them to volunteer their services to the fight against racial discrimination. A number of lawyers met the president's challenge and formed the Lawyers' Committee for Civil Rights Under Law, an organization which helps secure equal justice for all American citizens through pro bono litigation and public advocacy. Members of the committee have argued successfully before the Supreme Court in several voters' rights cases, and played a crucial role in the passage of the National Voter Registration Act in 1993. They have also fought on behalf of minority citizens to combat discrimination in public housing and education and at the workplace.

The Lawyers' Committee filed a lawsuit in a Virginia circuit court in April 2002, alleging that a redrawing of the state's 4th Congressional district violated the Voting Rights Act. By reducing the eligible minority voting population of the district to 33.6 percent, the committee argued, the state legislature had adversely affected the ability of black voters to elect a candidate of their choice. They withdrew the suit in November 2002, but planned to refile in the federal court system in time to have the case resolved before the 2004 elections. The committee also collaborated with the NAACP in an investigation into the redistricting of Boston, Mass., after residents of Mattapan, a neighborhood with a large black population, complained that they had not been granted sufficient input into the changes to their district.

The Lawyers' Committee was part of a legal team that helped six students from public schools in and near Holyoke, Mass., file a federal lawsuit in September 2002 against city and state education officials over Massachusetts Comprehensive Assessment System exams in English and math, which all students must pass in order to graduate. The six students are all members of the class of 2003, the first required to take the 10th grade exams mandated by education reform legislation in 1993. Their lawyers argue that they haven't been adequately prepared for the tests by their school systems, and that the tests themselves discriminate against minority students and those with limited English skills.

GETTING HIRED

The Lawyers' Committee web site, www.lawyerscomm.org, has job openings and contact information (you'll have to mail your cover letter, resume and writing sample to the Washington, DC headquarters). The Committee prefers attorneys with civil rights litigation experience, but recent law school grads may be able to make up the difference if they demonstrate sufficiently strong writing, research and analytic skills. There's an unpaid internship program for those still in school. Recent graduates can apply for the George N. Lindsay Civil Rights Fellowship, a one-year program that provides a $42,000 stipend, a $2,000 payment on school loans, and pays for bar review and fees. The competition for the fellowship is in some ways even tougher than that for a staff position; you'll be called upon to identify specific goals for your year with the Committee and outline a plan for how to achieve them.

The Committee prefers attorneys with civil rights litigation experience.

Legal Aid Society of New York

One Battery Park Plaza
New York, NY 10004
Phone: (212) 577-3300
www.legal-aid.org

LOCATIONS

New York, NY *

25 locations through the city's five boroughs

MAJOR DEPARTMENTS & PRACTICES

Civil
Criminal Appeals
Criminal Defense
Juvenile Rights

THE STATS

No. of attorneys: 900
No. of other employees: 1,700
Chair: Frederick P. Schaffer
President/Attorney-in-Chief: Daniel L. Greenberg

EMPLOYMENT CONTACT

Civil
Marie Richardson
The Legal Aid Society
199 Water Street
New York, NY 10038

Criminal Defense
Susan Hendricks
The Legal Aid Society
One Battery Park Plaza
New York, NY 10004

Juvenile Rights
Monica Drinane
The Legal Aid Society
304 Park Avenue South
Brooklyn, NY 10010

BASE SALARY

Entry-level: $41,200 before passing the bar, $41,973 after passing the bar

THE SCOOP

Lawyers for the poor

Founded in 1876, the Legal Aid Society of New York is the nation's oldest legal services organization. It's also the country's largest public interest law firm, with 900 attorneys handling over 300,000 cases a year. More than two-thirds of that caseload stems from defense services for indigent persons facing criminal charges throughout New York City's five boroughs, including the work of the Federal Defender Division, which represents financially strapped defendants in the U.S. District Courts for New York's Southern and Eastern Districts. Task forces within the Society's ranks are devoted exclusively to capital defense cases, ex-offenders charged with parole violations and prisoners' rights, and recently initiated programs that provide assistance to criminal defense clients with a history of mental illness or criminal addiction. Each of the Society's three major practice areas – Criminal, Juvenile Rights, and Civil – also has a specialized unit that focuses on class action and law reform litigation and appeals.

The Legal Aid Society was one of the first public interest law firms to represent juvenile clients, and pioneered the collaboration between public interest attorneys and social workers. Today, the agency handles 90 percent of the cases in New York City's Family Court. They provide minors with legal representation in cases of child abuse and neglect, as well as representing them in juvenile delinqunecy proceedings and, when minors are tried as adults, providing them with criminal defense attorneys. One recent example: on April 11, 2002, shortly after his arrival at LaGuardia Airport, 12-year-old Prince Nnaedozie Umegbolu developed severe stomach cramps. When police discovered the cramps were caused by having swallowed 87 condoms full of heroin, they arrested Prince for drug possession. Although Umbegbolu was eventually able to retain private counsel, the Legal Aid Society provided Umegbolu with representation during the early phases of his case, unsuccessfully petitioning to have the boy removed from incarceration and placed into the custody of his mother (a Georgia resident).

The Civil Division is the oldest of the Society's three major practices, reaching back to 1876, when a single lawyer worked part-time to assist newly arrived immigrants confused about their rights under American law. Today, client services are provided through a network of neighborhood offices in each borough, as well as special citywide units focusing on specific areas of civil law, including advocating for the homeless and immigrant and consumer law practice. The division serves a wide range of clients, from the unemployed and disabled to homeless families and people with AIDS. They also run a Community Law Office with a full-time staff of lawyers and paralegals serving the East Harlem community. The East Harlem office is the center of the Volunteer Division, which coordinates efforts with lawyers from private firms and corporate law departments eager to do pro bono work.

After September 11, the agency helped provide legal assistance to many who lived and worked near Ground Zero, as well as others affected by the disaster. The Society also collaborated with local labor unions on assisting workers and worked with service organizations to establish the World Trade Center Small Business Relief Project.

GETTING HIRED

The Legal Aid Society's web site, www.legal-aid.org, has contacts for attorneys interested in its three major practice areas (criminal defense, civil and juvenile rights). Legal Aid also offers unpaid internships both during the summer and academic year.

Legal Aid offers unpaid internships both during the summer and the academic year.

Los Angeles County District Attorney

210 West Temple Street
Los Angeles, CA 90012
Phone: (213) 974-3512
http://da.co.la.ca.us/

LOCATIONS

Los Angeles, CA

THE STATS

No. of attorneys: 1,035
No. of other employees: 2,261
District Attorney: Steve Cooley

BASE SALARY

1st year: $53,300

EMPLOYMENT CONTACT

Office of the District Attorney
Human Resources Division
201 North Figueroa Street
Suite1300
Los Angeles, CA 90012

THE SCOOP

To enforce the law

The Los Angeles County District Attorney's Office, which began as a one-man operation in 1850, has become the largest prosecutor's office in the United States, employing over 1,000 deputy district attorneys. The office filed over 56,400 felony complaints in 2001 and obtained 39 grand jury indictments, but with less than 300 criminal courtrooms in the county, very few of the cases actually make it to trial.

Trials of the rich and famous

Former television star Robert Blake was arrested on April 18, 2002, and charged with murder in the shooting death of his wife, Bonny Lee Bakley. Because the charge included special circumstances of lying in wait, a capital offense in California, he was denied a bail hearing prior to his preliminary hearing, scheduled towards the end of the year. Since prosecutors had already announced that they would not seek the death penalty, Blake's defense attorney, who had previously alleged that he had been arrested as a publicity boost for the city's outgoing police chief, pressed the state Supreme Court to order a bail hearing. The hearing took place, and bail was denied. Shortly afterwards, police recovered two guns, ammunition and other objects stored in a gym bag from a barn on Blake's property, identifying the items as potential evidence in the related charges of conspiracy and solicitation to commit murder.

In the year's other major celebrity case, Winona Ryder's shoplifting charges finally went to trial in October. The actress was arrested after being accused of stealing over $5,500 worth of clothing and accessories from a Saks Fifth Avenue outlet in Beverly Hills. After a two-week trial, jurors found Ryder guilty of grand theft and vandalism charges, but cleared her on a burglary count.

Busting bad cops

Nino Durden, one of the nine members of the LAPD's Rampart Division to be prosecuted after allegations of widespread misconduct and corruption throughout the department, was sentenced in August 2002 to five years in state prison for conspiring to obstruct justice, perjury, grand theft and filing a false police report. Durden, one of seven officers convicted in the Rampart scandal, admitted to shooting Javier Francisco Ovando and planting a gun on him, then lying about it in court to secure a prison sentence for the unarmed victim. He also confessed to several other crimes committed with the help of his former partner, who had been granted immunity in the Ovando case in exchange for testimony implicating nearly 70 other officers.

GETTING HIRED

Prospective deputy district attorneys at the Los Angeles DA's office must submit their applications to the office's human resources department from mid-October through mid-December (candidates can also apply in person). Applications are available at the DA's web site, da.co.la.ca.us. Deputy district attorneys must be admitted to the California bar and must have a valid driver's license. Expect a background check to weed out those with felony convictions and work-related misdemeanors.

The Los Angeles County District Attorney's Office is the largest prosecutor's office in the United States, employing over 1,000 deputy district attorneys.

Mexican American Legal Defense and Educational Fund

634 S. Spring Street
Los Angeles, CA 90014
Phone: (213) 629-2512
www.maldef.org

EMPLOYMENT CONTACT

http://www.maldef.org/about/
employment.cfm

LOCATIONS

Los Angeles, CA (HQ)
Albuquerque, NM
Atlanta, GA
Chicago, IL
Houston, TX
Phoenix, AZ
Sacramento, CA
San Antonio, TX
Washington DC

MAJOR DEPARTMENTS & PRACTICES

Civil Rights
Criminal Justice
Employment Discrimination
Immigration

THE STATS

No. of attorneys: 18
No. of other employees: 75
President: Antonio Hernandez
Vice President, Legal Program:
Thomas A. Saenz

THE SCOOP

In 1968 members of the League of United Latin American Citizens established the Mexican American Legal Defense and Educational Fund (MALDEF) to promote Latino civil rights through litigation and public advocacy. Originally based in San Antonio, Texas, MALDEF soon relocated, first to San Francisco and then to Los Angeles. (They've kept a regional office in San Antonio, though, and have since expanded to seven other cities.) In 1982 the group successfully argued Plyler v. Doe before the Supreme; the decision established the right of children of undocumented workers to a public education. They have also mounted legal battles to protect Latinos from discrimination in the workplace and at the voting booths, as well as education initiatives aimed at keeping the Latino community apprised of its rights.

The current head of MALDEF, Antonia Hernandez, has been with the organization since 1981, when she became the regional counsel for the DC office. Before that, she worked at the Los Angeles Center for Law and Justice and served as counsel to the Senate Judiciary Committee.

Higher education

Although Plyler v. Doe secured the right to receive a public education up to the twelfth grade, it offers no guarantee for admission into state colleges or universities. Although many states have passed laws that allow illegal immigrants to enroll in state colleges at in-state tuition rates, the Virginia attorney general's office decided in November 2002 to order the state's public colleges to refuse any such applications and report illegal immigrants found on campus to federal authorities. MALDEF was critical of the new directive, pointing out that it denied illegal immigrants the opportunity to acquire skills and knowledge that could help them become productive members of society. They also underscored the potential for racial profiling of legal immigrants. Staffers at the attorney general's office defended the policy, claiming that it preserved spots in the Virginia higher education system for legitimate state citizens and citing the increased security risks illegal immigrants might pose in the post-September 11 era.

That same month, MALDEF joined forces with the Midwest Immigrant and Human Rights Center to file a federal lawsuit against the Immigration and Naturalization Service, accusing the agency of violating the rights of thousands of illegal immigrants in the Chicago area over a four-year period. The allegation stems from a change in the way the Chicago branch office handled improper applications from immigrants seeking legal status. Originally, employees would hand forms back to unqualified applicants without comment, but in 1998, the agency decided to deport illegal aliens discovered through the applications. MALDEF argued that the policy shift helped enable deceptive "immigration consultants," known as notarios, to defraud immigrants by persuading them to file improper paperwork.

Where's the money going?

In October 2002, MALDEF addressed members of the California Children and Families Commission, which oversees the spending of funds collected by a 50-cent tax on each pack of cigarettes sold within the state. The money is supposed to provide child care and early education services to children five years and under, but MALDEF suggested that the state's Latino children were not reaping the full benefits of the tax. Surveying the 14 counties with the highest Latino populations, they discovered that although Latinos make up a majority of the young population in over half the counties, only 24 percent of those children eligible had enrolled in preschool or kindergarten. They recommended that the commission conduct increased demographic research on the recipients of services provided through the funds.

GETTING HIRED

MALDEF's web site, www.maldef.org, has an employment section that includes job opportunities at its Los Angeles headquarters and its branch offices. An interest in and/or experience with immigration law is preferred, as is a passion for civil rights issues. Legislative experience and aggressive networking and organizational skills are also looked upon favorably.

At MALDEF, an interest in and/or experience with immagration law is preferred, as is a passion for civil rights issues.

Manhattan District Attorney

One Hogan Place
New York, NY 10013
Phone: (212) 335-9000
www.manhattanda.org

LOCATIONS

New York, NY

THE STATS

No. of attorneys: 550
No. of other employees: 1250
District Attorney: Robert M. Morgenthau

BASE SALARY

1st year: $47,500

EMPLOYMENT CONTACT

Robin R. Edwards
Administrator of the Legal Hiring Unit
New York County District Attorney's
 Office
One Hogan Place
New York, NY 10013
Phone: (212) 335-9361

THE SCOOP

Cleaning up the Big Apple

Law and Order has had three different district attorneys in 12 seasons, but the real life Manhattan District Attorney's office has had significantly less turnover - the current chief prosecutor, Robert Morgenthau, was first elected in 1974, and his predecessor, Frank Hogan, lasted 32 years in the hot seat. That kind of stability comes in handy when you're handling 130,000 criminal cases every year.

For many, the Central Park Jogger case summed up the lawlessness of New York City in the late 1980s and early 1990s. In two highly publicized trials, five teens were convicted of assaulting and raping a woman, then leaving her for dead, during a nightlong crime spree in the park. The suspects were convicted largely on videotaped confessions. In 2002, Matias Reyes, who was in prison for four other rapes committed soon after the Central Park case but had never been a suspect, told authorities that he had attacked the victim alone. A reinvestigation of the DNA evidence corroborated his story, and the district attorney's office reopened the case and ultimately vacated the original guilty verdicts, despite protests by the police department.

World Trade Center fraud

Fifteen people were charged in June 2002 with stealing from charities, or attempting to file fraudulent claims, in the aftermath of the September 11 terrorist attack on the World Trade Center. Three women, for example, falsely claimed that they had been laid off from their jobs at the New York City Housing Authority and applied to the Red Cross and the Federal Emergency Management Agency for financial aid. They were only a few of the nearly 100 indictments the Manhattan district attorney's office had brought on such charges.

The DA's office scored back-to-back victories against sales tax cheats in October 2002. The manager of the National Arts Club's dining room pled guilty to skimming more than $160,000 in sales taxes over a three-year period. The very next day, Baron Andreas von Zadora-Gerlof confessed to evading $651,370 in taxes from the sale of elaborate gem sculptures. The artist, who sold his work out of a Fifth Avenue showroom, would frequently deliver commissioned pieces to New York clients and then ship empty boxes to out-of-state locations to avoid incurring sales taxes; DA Morgenthau announced that his office would continue to investigate the possibility of filing charges against his customers for their involvement in such transactions.

Martinizing

In 1921, the New York state legislature passed a securities law, the Martin Act, which gives the state's attorneys even more authority to prosecute corporate fraud than the federal government would later provide the Securities and Exchange Commission. (In addition to a broad definition of what constitutes the fraudulent sale of securities, the state law doesn't require proof of intent to defraud.) The Manhattan District Attorney's office has used the Martin Act aggressively since the mid-1990s, and in September 2002 they put together a case that rivals Enron and WorldCom for headline-grabbing potential, bringing indictments against former Tyco executives L. Dennis Kozlowski and Mark H. Swartz. The two were charged with granting themselves $170 million in unauthorized bonuses and selling $430 million worth of stock while concealing information from the company's other investors. The probe later expanded to include Tyco's former auditors at PricewaterhouseCoopers.

In March 2002, the DA's office won Martin Act convictions against owners of three franchises of the defunct securities firm Meyer Pollock. Operating without corporate supervision, according to the DA's press release, the three "taught their brokers how to sell securities by fraud," handpicked the stocks to sell, and created a false paper trail to cover up their activities, while an employee bought and sold stocks to manipulate their price without customer authorization. In addition to the Martin Act violations, the three were also convicted on several other counts, including enterprise corruption and grand larceny, while the employee got off comparatively light, with only a single conviction for scheming to defraud.

GETTING HIRED

The Manhattan District Attorney's office does not accept e-mail or faxed applications; all resumes and cover letters must be sent to the legal hiring administrator in New York. The DA recruits at over 40 campuses and job fairs on the East Coast. The odds aren't in your favor. The DA gets approximately 1,600 applicants every year for 50 to 60 openings.

Applicants can expect four rounds of interviews. After the initial screening interview, a prospective assistant DA will meet with three members of the hiring board, then the director of legal hiring. The final interview is with District Attorney Morgenthau. The DA offers a summer program that pays $500 a week. Law students can also apply to the Complaint Room Complex, where they help the assistant district attorneys draft misdemeanor complaints.

National Association for the Advancement of Colored People

4805 Mount Hope Drive
Baltimore, MD 21215
Phone: (877) 622-2798
www.naacp.org

EMPLOYMENT CONTACT

http://www.naacp.org/work
(877) 611-1798

LOCATIONS

Baltimore, MD (HQ)
81 branch offices nationwide

MAJOR DEPARTMENTS & PRACTICES

Civil Rights
Voters' Rights

THE STATS

President: Kweisi Mfume

THE SCOOP

Fighting for racial justice

On February 12, 1909, a group of African American civil rights leaders, including W.E.B. DuBois, formed the National Negro Committee, which soon renamed itself the National Association for the Advancement of Colored People (NAACP). For nearly a century, they have been on the front lines of the civil rights movement, from anti-lynching efforts during the 1910s to the fight for voter rights after the 2000 presidential elections. Supreme Court Justice Thurgood Marshall started out as a lawyer for the organization, fighting segregation in the nation's public schools, and was their lead counsel in the landmark Brown v. Board of Education case.

Today, as the African-American community has gone through several changes in the way it chooses to identify itself, the group is referred to almost exclusively by its title's acronym: NAACP. Prior to assuming leadership of the organization in 1996, Kweisi Mfume had served as the U.S. Representative for Maryland's 7th Congressional District, which includes portions of Baltimore, for 10 years. He has also been a radio and television host and authored a best selling memoir, *No Free Ride*.

The NAACP filed a federal lawsuit on behalf of nine current and former employees of the Florida Department of Corrections (FDC) who claimed that they had been subjected to discrimination on the job at three state prisons. During a two-week trial, they laid out their case, which included being passed over for promotion, forced to work the worst shifts, and subjected to racial slurs by co-workers and supervisors. The FDC's attorney argued that their problems were the result of personal disputes, not racism, and the jury apparently agreed, finding in the prison system's favor in November 2002.

On the road again

A federal judge in the Northern District of Georgia dealt a minor setback to the NAACP in October 2002 by denying class-action status to a lawsuit filed against Cracker Barrel Old Country Store Inc., a national chain of highway restaurants and gift shops. The suit had been filed in 2002 by 21 plaintiffs who accused Cracker Barrel outlets in 30 states of blatant discrimination, including segregated seating and shabby treatment of African-American customers. The NAACP had joined the case a few months later, along with several other defendants. The ruling did not end the lawsuit, but merely asserted that the plaintiffs had shown insufficient evidence to justify national class-action status.

The decision came shortly after South Carolina Attorney General Charlie Condon publicly announced his decision to drop a lawsuit against the NAACP over a series of protests held at state rest stops beginning in March 2002. The organization had begun conducting "border patrol" demonstrations aimed at discouraging travelers from spending money in the state as long as it continued to display the Confederate flag on Statehouse grounds. Condon noted that the NAACP's demonstrations had not led to any violence and hadn't done any substantial damage to the state's economy, so he felt no need to spend further money on unnecessary litigation.

Voters' rights

After the chaos of the Florida elections in 2000, many groups complained that African-American voters had been prevented from voting. The problems were blamed primarily on faulty election equipment and bungled voter registration procedures, including the accidental removal of eligible voters from the registration lists during a computerized search for convicted felons. The NAACP was one of several civil rights groups that filed a lawsuit against several state and county agencies in 2001 just as George W. Bush was assuming the office he'd won based on the disputed Florida results. Some of the defendants settled early, but it wasn't until September 2002 that the case was fully resolved. In addition to restoring the voting rights of citizens improperly turned away from the polls in 2000, Florida officials agreed to provide increased training for election workers and to strengthen its compliance with the National Voter Registration Act.

GETTING HIRED

For information about career openings at the NAACP, contact the national headquarters in Baltimore. You can call them toll-free at (877) 611-1798.

Supreme Court Justice Thurgood Marshall started out as a lawyer for the NAACP, and was their lead counsel in the landmark *Brown v. Board of Education* case.

National Asian Pacific American Legal Consortium

1140 Connecticut Avenue, NW
Suite 1200
Washington, DC 20036
Phone: (202) 296-2300
www.napalc.org

LOCATIONS

Washington, DC (HQ)

MAJOR DEPARTMENTS & PRACTICES

Affirmative Action
Anti-Asian Violence
Immigration and Naturalization
Language Rights
Voting Rights
Welfare Reform

THE STATS

No. of attorneys: 4
No. of other employees: 11
President: Karen K. Narasaki
Legal Director: Vincent A. Eng

EMPLOYMENT CONTACT

Vincent Eng
Legal Director
E-mail: veng@napalc.org

THE SCOOP

Civil rights mega-merger

Three Asian American and Pacific American advocacy groups from Los Angeles, San Francisco and New York teamed up in 1991 to found the National Asian Pacific American Legal Consortium (NAPALC). The group, which opened an office in Washington, DC, in 1993, promotes legal and civil rights for Pacific Americans through public education and lobbying as well as litigation. Their current director, Karen Narasaki, was selected as one of the 100 most powerful women in Washington by *Washingtonian* magazine in 2001. Before joining NAPALC, she ran the national advocacy program for the Japanese American Citizens League.

Backlash

NAPALC issued a report, "Backlash: When American Turned on Its Own," in March 2002, documenting the racial violence faced by many Asian and Pacific Americans after September 11, especially Sikhs, Indians and Pakistanis. (The victims were targeted because they were mistakenly identified as Middle Eastern and deemed "responsible" for the attacks.) The group also warned against the threat of bias posed by new government policies and an increased trend towards racial profiling among law enforcement agencies. A few months later, NAPALC issued a public criticism of the government's plan to incorporate the Immigration and Naturalization Service (INS) into its proposed Department of Homeland Security. They argued that such a move would hamper the ability of the INS to fully serve the nation's immigrants and unnecessarily burden anti-terrorist efforts. Despite the lobbying efforts of NAPALC, the Department of Homeland Security, including the INS, was approved and signed into law in November 2002.

Airport security

When the federal Transportation Security Administration (TSA) began taking over checkpoints at the nation's airports, many groups were angered by a new regulation requiring security screeners to hold U.S. citizenship. Although no precise figures were available, it was generally acknowledged that the pre-September 11 security teams, hired by private contractors, consisted largely of minority workers. The TSA workforce, by contrast, was 61 percent white.

NAPALC joined the legal team of nine former security screeners – eight permanent legal residents and a U.S. national from American Samoa – who filed a lawsuit against Transportation Secretary Norman Mineta to get their jobs back.

GETTING HIRED

NAPALC's web site, at www.napalc.org, has information about job vacancies at the organization. It also provides details on the internships available to law students; legal interns help staff attorneys research civil rights cases, draft amicus briefs and public statements, track legislation and engage in grassroots activism. Candidates need to have completed at least one semester of law school and provide a three- to five-page writing sample.

NAPALC internship candidates need to have completed at least one semester of law school and provide a three- to five-page writing sample.

National Association of State PIRGs

218 D Street, SE
Washington, DC 20003
Phone: (202) 546-9707
www.uspirg.org

LOCATIONS

Albequerque, NM • Ann Arbor, MI
• Atlanta, GA • Austin, TX •
Baltimore, MD • Boston, MA •
Chapel Hill, NC • Chicago, IL •
Cleveland, OH • Columbus, OH •
Concord, NH • Denver, CO • Des
Moines, IA • Harrisburg, PA •
Hartford, CT • Los Angeles, CA •
Madison, WI • New Orleans, LA •
Philadelphia, PA • Portland, ME •
Portland, OR • Providence, RI •
Sacramento, CA • St. Louis, MO •
Salt Lake City, UT • San Francisco,
CA • Santa Barbara, CA • Seattle,
WA • Tallahassee, FL • Trenton,
NJ • Washington, DC

PRACTICE AREAS

Campaign Finance Reform
Consumer & Health Care Law
Environmental Law
Public Policy

THE STATS

No. of attorneys: 24
No. of other staff: 418
Board Chair: Doug Phelps
Associate Political Director:
Kimberley Larson

EMPLOYMENT CONTACT

Moire Murray
Hiring Coordinator
29 Temple Place
Boston, MA 02111
E-mail: careers@pirg.org
Phone: (617) 747-4360
Fax: (617) 292-8057

http://www.pirg.org/jobs/recentgrads/

http://www.pirg.org/jobs/experienced/
Index.html

BASE SALARY

Starting salary is $26,000 and up,
depending on level of experience.

THE SCOOP

For the people

Consumer advocate Ralph Nader helped launch the public interest research group (PIRG) movement in the 1970s as a way of getting college students involved in public advocacy and activism. Using the same methods of investigative research and media outreach that Nader employed, plus litigation where appropriate, PIRGs have come to play a critical role in creating awareness about public health risks, environmental dangers and corporate abuses. Today, the National Association of State PIRGs unites public interest research groups in all 50 states and Washington, DC Attorneys at each PIRG are quickly given responsibility to craft their own issue agendas, and find themselves drafting legislation, organizing support, lobbying political leaders, and speaking to the media.

While most of the legal challenges to the campaign finance reform bill focused on its tightened restrictions on "soft money" contributions, three state PIRGs joined the national association in filing a lawsuit challenging the increased allowances for "hard money," which raise the maximum individual contribution to a political candidate to $2,000. In their legal complaint, filed in May 2002, the groups argue that the new limits violate the Fifth Amendment by denying poorer voters "the equal opportunity to participate in all integral aspects of the electoral process" by making it harder for them to gain access to candidates.

Fighting pollution

The Ohio PIRG joined forces with environmental law firm Earthjustice to file a lawsuit against the Environmental Protection Agency (EPA) in October 2002 demanding that it enforce the Clean Air Act in the state. The groups complained that the state's environmental protection agency, despite a previous warning from the federal government, failed to adequately protect its citizens from air pollution. State environmental officials insisted that they had stepped up their efforts after the EPA's 2001 findings.

The Northwest Environmental Law Center sued the owners of a surimi processing plant in Warrenton, Ore., in July 2002, after the Oregon State PIRG raised an outcry about the plant's alleged disposal of wastewater into the Skipanon River. The research group claimed that the discharged waste, which includes unused fish parts, oil and grease, suffocated the river's salmon and steelhead fish population. The suit further alleged that Pacific Coast Seafoods didn't even have a permit from the state's Department of Environmental Quality (DEQ) to discharge waste at the plant. The company responded to the suit by noting that the DEQ had given it a consent order to continue operations while it made improvements to the facility that would bring it into full compliance with state and federal regulations.

Gone fishin'

U.S. PIRG investigated claims that three Maine salmon farms, which accounted for roughly three-fourths of the state's growing salmon aquaculture industry, were discharging pollutants into the ocean without EPA permits. With help from the New England Law Center and National Environmental Law Center, they launched a federal lawsuit against the three companies, but reached a settlement with Heritage Salmon in June 2002. In the agreement, Heritage acknowledged operating without a Clean Water Act permit and agreed to evade the potential fines by donating money to efforts to restore the population of the endangered wild Atlantic salmon. The firm, which had already applied for a state Department of Environmental Protection permit, also agreed to tag all of their fishes so they could be identified if they escaped outside Heritage's pens and to refrain from raising genetically modified fishes. The suit against the remaining two companies is pending.

GETTING HIRED

The association's web site, www.pirg.org, lists job opportunities at each of the state PIRGs, including specific areas of focus like consumer advocacy or environmental law. There are numerous opportunities for grad students to do internships that offer direct experience in advocacy and litigation work under the close mentorship of experienced PIRG staff. In addition to a strong commitment to public interest issues, you'll need to prove that you can think fast on your feet and express your views articulately.

There are numerous opportunities for grad students to do internships that offer direct experience in advocacy and litigation work.

National Women's Law Center

11 Dupont Circle, NW
Suite 800
Washington, DC 20036
Phone: (202) 588-5180
www.nwlc.org

LOCATIONS

Washington, DC

THE STATS

No. of attorneys: 25
Total no. of employees: 40
Co-Presidents: Marcia D.
Greenberger and Nancy Duff
Campbell

EMPLOYMENT CONTACT

Human Resources Department
National Women's Law Center
11 Dupont Circle, NW
Suite 800
Washington, DC 20036
Fax: (202) 588-5185
E-mail: humanresources@nwlc.org

THE SCOOP

For women, by women

The National Women's Law Center (NWLC) was founded in 1972 when female administrative staff at the Center for Law and Social Policy demanded that the firm start hiring women attorneys. The new hires quickly made major legal advances for women's rights in America's courts and legislatures, and looked for ways not just to take the cause further, but to teach other women about the opportunities opening up for them.

Their practice today covers a wide range of women's issues, concentrated in four distinct practice areas which focus on raising public awareness as well as on litigation and public policy research. The education program works to ensure gender equity, particularly with adherence to Title IX, the federal civil rights law banning sex discrimination in the education system (not just, as prominent cases often lead people to believe, school atheltics). The Employment program fights for affordable, high-quality child care for working mothers, combats sexual harassment and helps ensure women receive pay and benefits equal to their male counterparts in the workplace. The Health program deals with reproductive rights, but also emphasizes the need for increased access to health care and for advanced research on women's health issues. And the Family Economic Security program calls attention to the need for programs and policies that can help economically disadvantaged women — including single mothers, women of color, and older women.

Fighting for the pill

At NWLC's urging, the Equal Employment Opportunities Commission (EEOC) ruled in December 2000 that an employer's failure to cover prescription contraceptives in its otherwise comprehensive health insurance plan constitutes unlawful sex discrimination. Several months later, in a case in Seattle in which the National Women's Law Center was involved, the first federal court to rule on the issue made a similar finding. The NWLC is currently working on a case to get coverage of prescription contraceptives for Wal-Mart employees.

On another front, when several female law students at George Washington University became upset because birth control pills were not available through their student health plan, the NWLC, along with Planned Parenthood and a local public interest law firm, wrote to the university's administration arguing that this lack of coverage constituted sexual discrimination under applicable federal and local laws. The university decided not to fight the issue, and announced in August 2002 that, while they did not feel legally bound to do so, they would be adding coverage for prescription contraceptives because "this was something students wanted."

GETTING HIRED

You can search for job openings on the NWLC's web site, www.nwlc.org, and submit your application materials by e-mail. They also encourage law students and recent graduates to consider basing a fellowship project at the center, and will discuss sponsoring applications for fellowships from New York-based law firm Skadden, Arps, Slate, Meagher & Flom, Equal Justice Works (formerly known as the National Association for Public Interest Law) and other organizations. Law students may also participate in NWLC's summer internship program, or earn course credits by interning during the semester. Second- or third-year students should consider the Chesterfield Smith internship, a 12-week program that pairs the intern up with an attorney mentor, offers a wide range of possible assignments and comes with a small stipend.

Law students may earn course credits by interning during the semester.

Nuclear Regulatory Commission

11545-11555 Rockville Pike
Rockville, MD 20852
Phone: (301) 415-8200
www.nrc.gov

LOCATIONS

Rockville, MD (HQ)
Arlington, TX
Atlanta, GA
Chattanooga, TN
King of Prussia, PA
Las Vegas, NV
Lisle, IL

MAJOR DEPARTMENTS & PRACTICES

Licensing and Regulation
Legislation
Materials Mitigation and
    Enforcement
Reactor Programs
Rulemaking and Fuel Cycle

THE STATS

No. of attorneys: 88
No. of other employees: 2,842
Chairman: Richard A. Meserve
General Counsel: Karen D. Cyr

EMPLOYMENT CONTACT

Mary Ann Warner
Office of General Counsel
U.S. Nuclear Regulatory Commission
Washington, DC 20555
E-mail: maw@nrc.gov

BASE SALARY

1st Year: $61,376 (GS-11, Step 9,
including Washington, DC locality pay)

THE SCOOP

In charge of the atom

In the 1950s, Congress authorized the Atomic Energy Commission (AEC) to both encourage the development of newly available commercial nuclear power and regulate its safety. Critics believed that the AEC's efforts to promote the industry negatively affected their ability to impose strict guidelines on its growth, and attacked its standards for assessing public safety and environmental impact. Congress responded by shutting down the commission and creating two separate groups in its place, opening the Nuclear Regulatory Commission (NRC) for business in January 1975. The NRC primarily concerns itself with monitoring the companies to whom it grants licenses for the operation of nuclear power plants, the handling of nuclear materials for use in reactors and other facilities, and the disposal of nuclear waste.

An employee at an Exelon nuclear plant in Illinois spoke out about a potential safety problem, and believed that he was deliberately passed over for a promotion as a result. After investigating his complaint, the NRC agreed that Exelon had violated regulations that prohibit its licensees from "punishing" employees for bringing up safety issues. The employee involved was no longer at the plant after a company-wide layoff, but Exelon agreed to retrain management at its 21 nuclear plants about the employee protection regulations.

Where can we put this?

In April 2002, Nevada state officials filed a lawsuit against the NRC regarding the commission's ruling on a license for storing nuclear waste at a site in Yucca Mountain, Nev. The suit claimed the NRC (and the Department of Energy, the original target of the complaint) ignored rules on granting a waste storage license to Yucca Mountain. Yucca Mountain has been selected as the final resting place for nuclear waste produced in the U.S., a decision many in Nevada are resisting.

Until Yucca Mountain opens for business, many nuclear plants have no option but to store their radioactive waste on site. Carolina Power & Light received permission from the NRC to build two new cooling pools at the Shearon Harris facility in Orange County, N.C., bringing the total number of pools at the site to four. Lawyers for Orange County filed a lawsuit against the commission, claiming they had not done sufficient research on the environmental impact of the plans or the threat of statewide contamination should the pools partially drain and allow the waste to catch fire. The two parties argued their cases before the DC Circuit Court of Appeals in September 2002.

GETTING HIRED

The NRC hires a limited number of exceptional law graduates for the Honors Law Graduates program. The commission looks for law grads in the top 30 percent of their class (though students below that threshold with other graduate degrees or interesting work experience are considered) for the two-year program. Honors attorneys rotate through four or five divisions during the two years and are permitted to stay on in a permanent position without reapplying. The Office of General Counsel also offers a paid summer internship program. Like most government agencies, the NRC conducts a thorough background check, but the commission has a "zero-tolerance" drug-use policy. See the NRC's web site, www.nrc.gov, for a career section with contact information and deadlines (usually mid-October for the Honors program).

"Honors attorneys rotate through four or five divisions during the two years and are permitted to stay on in a permanent position without reapplying."

Occupational Saftey and Health Administration

200 Constitution Avenue, NW
Washington, DC 20210
Phone: (202) 208-8663
www.osha.gov

LOCATIONS

Washington, DC (HQ)
Atlanta, GA
Boston, MA
Chicago, IL
Dallas, TX
Denver, CO
Kansas City, MO
New York, NY
Philadelphia, PA
San Francisco, CA
Seattle, WA

THE STATS

No. of employees: 2,316
Assistant Secretary of Labor,
OSHA: John L. Henshaw

BASE SALARY

1st year: $46,469

THE SCOOP

Safety first

The Occupational Safety and Health Administration (OSHA), a branch of the Department of Labor, was created in 1971 to address unsafe workplace conditions that were causing sharp increases in work-related deaths and disabling injuries. In its first 30 years of operation, the administration has set safety and health standards applying to nearly 7 million work sites nationwide. The agency's rules are credited with halving the number of occupation deaths (5,900 in 2001) and reducing injuries on the job by 40 percent. Even government agencies must comply to OSHA's regulations: In June 2002, a Houston branch of the U.S. Postal Service was cited for failing to protect its employees from protruding machine parts or exposed horizontal shafts and charged with a repeat violation for failing to provide sufficient clearance in passageways where mechanical equipment was used after having been cited for that offense less than three years ago.

In May 2002, Beverly Enterprises, which owns and operates over 500 nursing home across the country, reached an agreement with OSHA to purchase more ergonomically designed equipment and offer more training to its employees about avoiding back injuries while moving patients. The company had spent over $21 million to improve conditions at its facilities over a 10-year period, but agreed to accelerate its efforts to meet non-binding guidelines the administration was developing for the prevention of musculoskeletal disorders specific to the nursing home industry, which suffers from an abnormally high rate of worker-related injuries, after Congress repealed the ergonomics regulations the year before. OSHA published a draft version of those guidelines a few months later, and launched a national emphasis program in September, conducting comprehensive inspections at all nursing home facilities with worker injury rates of 14 percent or higher.

On April 25, 2002, an explosion in the basement of Kaltech Industries Group's Manhattan headquarters briefly revived residents' fears of terrorist attacks. OSHA conducted an immediate inspection of the site and, after months of deliberation, issued a 36-count citation against Kaltech in late October, with total penalties assessed at $88,000. The most serious violations included failing to label or properly store chemical containers, failing to educate employees about chemical hazards and failing to provide employees with protective bodywear or equipment.

Enforcement action

In two separate rulings in June 2002, OSHA fined employers for unsafe work conditions that led to workers losing parts of their hands. An Illinois company was fined $295,000 after an employee lost three fingers to a mechanical power press. The company was fined for failing to properly maintain and supervise the presses and for failing to train employees in their safe use. At a manufacturing facility in Wisconsin, an employee was trying to unclog a metering valve on a wood-grinding machine which had not been properly locked out from its power source. The valve moved unexpectedly, severing four fingers and most of the palm from the worker's right hand. OSHA determined that the firm did not have adequate power lockout procedures and issued a fine of $121,450.

In late October 2001, scaffolding at a Park Avenue renovation project in Manhattan collapsed, killing five immigrant construction workers. OSHA's investigation led to six citations and a proposed penalty of $146,600 against Tri-State Scaffolding for violations of scaffold safety rules, and citations against New Millennium Restoration for not providing its employees with adequate safety training or protective equipment. (Two weeks before the first anniversary of the incident, Tri-State's president was indicted by the Manhattan district attorney's office on five counts of second-degree manslaughter plus four counts of second-degree assault stemming from injuries to other workers.) The deaths also spurred OSHA to begin collecting data on country of origin and primary language for workers in fatal accidents to determine the role language barriers might play in accidents involving immigrant workers.

GETTING HIRED

OSHA's recruiting efforts are coordinated through its parent organization, the Department of Labor. Job vacancies are posted on OSHA's web site, www.osha.gov.

The administration has set safety and health standards applying to nearly 7 million work sites nationwide.

Office of the Comptroller of the Currency

250 E Street SW
Washington, DC 20219
Phone: (202) 874-4700
www.occ.treas.gov

LOCATIONS

Washington, DC (HQ)
Atlanta, GA
Chicago, IL
Dallas, TX
Kansas City, MO
New York, NY
San Francisco, CA
London, UK

THE STATS

No. of employees: 3,031
Comptroller of the Currency: John D. Hawke

UPPERS

- "No pressure" work environment
- "Compassionate" management

DOWNERS

- Slow, politically driven decision making process
- Little room for creativity

EMPLOYMENT CONTACT

Comptroller of the Currency
250 E Street, SW
Office of the Chief Counsel
Attention: Executive Assistant
Washington, DC 20219
Phone: (202) 874-5200

http://www.occ.treas.gov/jobs/lawjob.htm

THE SCOOP

Watching the money

Decades before the Federal Reserve Bank became the single source for American currency, Treasury Secretary Salmon P. Chase convinced President Lincoln of the importance of creating a standardized system for granting federal charters to banks that could issue currency notes. The National Currency Act of 1863 established the Office of the Comptroller of the Currency (OCC) to oversee this process. That law was eventually superseded by the National Bank Act, which gave the OCC extended authority to examine and regulate the banks to which it granted charters. It continues to fulfill these functions through the supervision of more than 2,200 federally chartered banks, comprising nearly 30 percent of the country's commercial banking system.

Credit card warnings

In June 2002 a federal court put on hold a California law requiring credit card companies to tell their customers how long it would take to pay off their balances making only the minimum monthly payment. Several of the nation's largest banks filed a joint lawsuit claiming that the expense of creating such notices would force them to raise the monthly minimums. Douglas Jordan, the OCC's senior counsel, spoke at the hearing to explain why this would violate federal regulations preventing states from interfering with bank's payment schedules or interest rates.

States are also prohibited, under the Gramm-Leach-Bliley Act of 1999, from interfering with the ability of a bank to sell, solicit, or cross-market insurance. The law does make exceptions for certain state law provisions, however, so the Massachusetts Bankers Association asked the OCC to determine whether three provisions of a Massachusetts law applied to national banks. After two years of deliberation, the OCC issued an opinion that the federal law would preempt Massachusetts from prohibiting employees of national banks from referring prospective customers to licensing insurance agents without being asked for a referral by the customer or prohibiting the bank from compensating the employee for the referral or from telling a loan applicant about available insurance products before the loan's approval.

Early paydays

The OCC has taken a particular interest in the problems associated with payday loans, short-term cash advances to consumers who provide the lender with a post-dated personal check. Although most payday loans are provided by check cashing outlets and other institutions which fall outside the OCC's authority, it can and does take action against national banks when appropriate. In March 2002 the OCC filed a notice of charges against the People's National Bank of Paris, Texas, alleging that it had allowed its payday lending program to expand to unsound levels – 240 percent of capital within the first eight months of operation. The bank also relied upon third-party service providers to administer the payday loans without fully determining whether the other companies could perform such operations effectively.

Similarly, the Goleta National Bank of Goleta, Calif., authorized ACE Cash Express to make and collect payday loans, under its charter, at branch offices in 18 states. But ACE's mismanagement of its customer loan files, including throwing 641 files at one branch into an unlocked trash dumpster, led to numerous violations of the Equal Credit Opportunity Act, requiring financial institutions to retain loan documents for 25 months, and the Truth in Lending Act. Goleta's failure to properly oversee ACE also violated several banking standards, including those for consumer privacy and information security. The OCC's investigation led to cease and desist orders against both companies, and further prohibits ACE from providing services to any other national bank without permission from the Comptroller's office.

War on terrorism

The OCC has been charged with keeping banks apprised of anti-terrorism legislation involving financial institutions. In October 2002, the OCC issued bulletins for two new regulations. One required financial institutions to comply "expeditiously" with requests from the Financial Crimes Enforcement Network and allowed limited communication between institutions about clients suspected of possible terrorist activity or money laundering. The other rule prohibits financial institutions from providing correspondent accounts to foreign shell banks.

GETTING HIRED

The OCC recruits third-year law students for the Office of Chief Counsel Employment Program on an as-needed basis. Competition for the positions is "keen," as one OCC attorney describes it, and students in the top quarter of their graduating class are preferred, as are those with relevant course work (securities law, financial services law, etc.), law review and financial work experience or judicial clerkships. Most applicants are interviewed in Washington, DC, but interviews occasionally take place at district offices in New York, Atlanta, Chicago, Dallas, Kansas City and San Francisco. "The law department recruits at select law schools" as well, notes one attorney, "but if you're really interested, don't wait for a campus visit, apply direct!" A stated intention to stay with the Comptroller's office at least three or four years will work strongly to your advantage. The OCC sometimes hires summer law interns but has no plans to do so for 2003. Deadline and contact information can be found at the OCC's web site, ww.occ.treas.gov.

OUR SURVEY SAYS

"A goverment agency is not going to be competitive with the private sector," one OCC attorney reminds us, but even so, "I still feel that our salaries remain uncompetitive with other [government] agencies. We do not receive bonuses and there is very little room for salary increases after you reach a certain grade level." Another attorney disagrees, saying lawyers at the OCC get "one of the best compensation packages for new government attorneys. If life balance is important to you, then the cash compensation and [benefits] plus intangibles (i.e., a real flexible work schedule, not just lip service) puts your compensation on par with the big dream firm."

"The OCC is very receptive to women in terms of hiring and promotion," one source says. Another insider confirms, "There are many women in leadership and managerial positions in the agency and law department." But although the agency supports the development of minority interest groups, which provide mentorship opportunities," staffers still note that "while we have representation in all categories, there is a noticeable lack of focus in these areas." The work environment is "very friendly," employees say, though, as one attorney puts it, "many lawyers in this family-friendly agency have young kids, so the socializing opportunities are not in overdrive. That said, on occasion, several attorneys get together for dinner, movies, theater or at each other's homes. Lunch is a big social ritual as well."

U.S. Patent and Trademark Office

General Information Services
Division
Crystal Plaza 3, Room 2C02
Washington, DC 20231

As of 5/1/2003, address will be:
P.O. Box 1450
Alexandria, VA 22313
Phone: (703) 308-4357
www.uspto.gov

LOCATIONS

Washington, DC (HQ)

MAJOR DEPARTMENTS & PRACTICES

Intellectual Property
Patent Law
Trademark Law

THE STATS

No. of attorneys: 250
No. of other employees: 6,749
Under Secretary of Commerce for Intellectual Property and Director of the United States Patent and Trademark Office: James E. Rogan
General Counsel: James Toupin

UPPERS

- Flexibility in work scheduling
- Autonomy in decision making

DOWNERS

- Lack of job security
- Difficulty balancing quality and quantity in patent review process

EMPLOYMENT CONTACT

http://www.uspto.gov/web/offices/ac/ahrpa/ohr/jobs/jobs.htm

THE SCOOP

200 years of patents

The United States Patent and Trademark Office (PTO) celebrated its bicentennial in the summer of 2002. America's earliest patent law, signed by George Washington in 1790, required inventors to petition the Secretary of State for patents which would, if the invention was determined "sufficiently useful and important," be approved by both the Secretary and the President. As the applications poured in, the State Department soon shifted the bulk of the workload to clerks, but it wasn't until 1802 that Dr. William Thornton was appointed specifically to supervise the processing of patent applications and issuing of patents. The office eventually assumed the second responsibility of registering trademarks and, after a brief period in the Department of the Interior, became part of the Department of Commerce in 1925.

PTO lawyers are becoming a rare breed. After a decade-long rise in trademark applications, which rose to 375,000 in 2000, the office saw a noticeable downturn and, once it determined that only 250,000 applications would be filed in 2002, decided it would have to lay off up to 124 of its examining attorneys. Although the National Treasury Employees Union made an effort to save its members from the "reduction in force," arguing that they were needed to handle the substantial backlog of applications still remaining, the pink slips went out as scheduled on July 30.

Welcome to the Digital Age

The PTO issues thousands of patents, each running at least 20 pages, every week, and has taken steps to reduce the paper flow by phasing out the printed records in favor of electronic databases. But the National Intellectual Property Researchers Association (NIPRA), fearing flaws in the electronic system, filed a lawsuit against the office's director, James Rogan, in August 2002 to halt the process. Although NIPRA doesn't dispute that the databases can be easier to search than the printed files, they believe that the databases are full of errors, and that the automated search tools currently in use fail to uncover much information that a search of paper records would turn up.

Radio waves

When QSC Audio Protects applied to the PTO for a trademark on their PowerWave amplifier system, the Bose Corporation, which sells $150 million worth of radios under the Wave and Acoustic Wave trademarks each year, complained that consumers would believe they made the amplifiers. The Office's Trademark Trial and Appeal Board rejected that argument, so Bose went to the Federal Circuit Court of Appeals, which agreed that "Wave" deserved extra trademark protection because of its recognition value. QSC responded to the decision with defiance, noting that it had been using the PowerWave name since 1994 without previous complaint, and held a California trademark as well.

GETTING HIRED

The PTO's web site, www.uspto.gov, has a career section that lists openings and has downloadable application forms, as well as contacts for legal positions. One attorney reports that the agency is currently in a hiring freeze and further cautions, "When they hire, it is usually someone who knows a person employed at the Office." Another staffer offers some advice for choosing which jobs you might apply for. "A patent examiner does not need a law degree," he reminds us. "Most don't have one. If you want to work as a real lawyer, don't be a patent examiner."

OUR SURVEY SAYS

"I had no interest in working somewhere where my contribution was measured by the number of hours that I work," says an administrative law judge who's been with the PTO for nearly a decade. The salary for new attorneys is much lower than it would be practicing the same type of law in the private sector, notes an attorney, who adds that "the starting salary immediately out of law school is too low for the Washington, DC metropolitan area." But the office culture is "very friendly" and offers employees broad freedom in setting their own work pace. "Normal work hours are 12 hours per day worked anytime between 5:30 a.m. and 11:30 p.m.," offers one source, who claims managers aren't especially concerned about when you work as long as you meet the biweekly requirement of 80 hours, so "I can work 20 hours the first week and 60 hours the second week."

"I can work 20 hours the first week and 60 hours the second week [to meet the biweekly requirement of 80 hours]."

— *U.S. Patent and Trademark Office attorney*

Security and Exchange Commission

450 Fifth Street, NW
Washington, DC 20549
Phone: (202) 942-7040
www.sec.gov

LOCATIONS

Washington, DC (HQ)
Atlanta, GA
Boston, MA
Chicago, IL
Denver, CO
Fort Worth, TX
Los Angeles, CA
Miami, FL
New York, NY
Philadelphia, PA
Salt Lake City, UT
San Francisco, CA

MAJOR DEPARTMENTS & PRACTICES

Corporation Finance
Enforcement
Market Regulation
Investment Management

THE STATS

No. of employees: 3,285
Chairman: William Donaldson

BASE SALARY

1st year: $60,000

EMPLOYMENT CONTACT

Candyce Pare
Summer Honors Program
U.S. Securities and Exchange
Commission
450 Fifth Street, NW
Washington, DC 20549-0801
Fax: (202) 942-9637

THE SCOOP

Making securities exchange secure

Congress created the Securities and Exchange Commission (SEC) in 1934 in response to the public's lack of faith in the capital markets following the crash of 1929. The SEC monitors public companies and the firms that sell or trade public securities. The agency's job seemed more urgent in late 2001 through early 2002, as several major corporations have collapsed due to years of deceptive practices on the part of top-level executives. The government has responded by giving the five-member commission increased authority to fight corporate fraud.

The Sarbanes-Oxley Act of 2002 had significant ramifications for corporate governance well beyond its extension of the statute of limitations on securities fraud to two years from the date of discovery or five years from the date of the violation. The new law requires any company making periodic statements containing financial information to accompany those statements with written certification by the CEO or CFO affirming they have accurately reported, "in all material respects, the financial condition and results of operation of the issuer," and also calls for a separate certification within 30 days after the filing of annual and quarterly reports. It also enables the SEC to propose regulations prohibiting professional auditors from offering other services, such as consulting, to the corporations they audit, and to prohibit the officers of such corporations from coercing their auditors into helping them make misleading statements.

Sarbanes-Oxley also established a Public Company Accounting Oversight Board to help establish and enforce stricter ethics and conflict-of-interest standards for accountants, discipline them for violations and conduct annual reviews of the nation's largest accounting firms. In late October 2002, SEC chairman Harvey Pitt selected William Webster, former head of the Federal Bureau of Investigation and the Central Intelligence Agency, to head the board, but the nomination was quickly thrown into dispute by Pitt's failure to inform fellow commissioners of Webster's participation in the audit committee of a struggling tech firm, U.S. Technologies, which stood accused of fraud. The controversy reinvigorated calls for Pitt's departure, and he resigned quietly, burying the announcement amidst election night results on November 5. Webster stepped down from the accounting oversight board a week later.

Martha Stewart living large

On December 27, 2001, Martha Stewart sold off her holdings in ImClone Systems, a biotechnology company founded by friend Samuel D. Waksal, as did two members of Waksal's family. At the close of trading the next day, ImClone announced that it had failed to obtain FDA approval for a cancer drug it had developed. An SEC investigation into the possibility of insider trading led to an August 2002 indictment against Waksal, who pled guilty in October to two counts of insider trading for telling his relatives to dump their stock, plus counts of obstruction of justice, perjury, bank fraud and conspiracy to obstruct justice and commit perjury (the last charge stemming from telling his daughter to lie to the SEC about his contact with her). That left two counts of conspiracy to commit securities fraud and five counts of insider trading on the original indictment, and the government expressed strong willingness to pursue the case, and made efforts to seize $10 million in assets belonging to Waksal's father and daughter.

Stewart, meanwhile, insisted that her trade was the result of a standing order to her stockbroker at Merrill Lynch, Peter Bacanovic, to dump ImClone if the price fell below $60. When the firm couldn't find any documentation for that order, it suspended Bacanovic; he was subsequently fired for his failure to cooperate with the investigation. Douglas Faneuil, his assistant, pled himself down to a misdemeanor in exchange for his cooperation, telling prosecutors that Stewart authorized the trade after Bacanovic informed her of the Waksal family's fire sale. In September 2002, the SEC formally notified Stewart that they had enough evidence to file a civil complaint, allowing Stewart to file a formal response before they made a final determination.

GETTING HIRED

The SEC offers an Advanced Commitment program for recent law school graduates and judicial clerks. The SEC recruits for Advanced Commitment candidates at select law schools. Students at other schools can send applications (including a cover letter, resume, transcript and five- to 10-page legal writing sample) to the Washington, DC headquarters or to the regional office of choice. Applicants should have "high academic qualifications" and knowledge of and interest in the securities industry.

First- and second-year law students can apply for the SEC's Summer Honors program, a 10-week rotation program in Washington and at regional offices.

The selection criteria is similar to the Advanced Commitment program, though the SEC does specify that second-years should have at least a B average.

The SEC recruits a significant number of experienced attorneys for all offices. Applications are accepted on an ongoing basis and should include a cover letter, resume, writing sample and law school transcript (for those with less than five years of experience).

Social Security Administration

6401 Security Blvd.
Baltimore, MD 21235
Phone: (800) 772-1213
www.ssa.gov

LOCATIONS

Washington, DC (HQ)
Atlanta, GA
Boston, MA
Chicago, IL
Dallas, TX
Denver, CO
Kansas City, MO
New York, NY
Philadelphia, PA
San Francisco, CA
Seattle, WA

MAJOR DEPARTMENTS & PRACTICES

Office of the General Counsel:
General Law
Litigation
Policy and Legislation

THE STATS

No. of other employees: 65,000
Commissioner: Jo Anne B. Barnhart
General Counsel: Lisa de Soto

http://www.ssa.gov/careers/legalcareer
s.htm

BASE SALARY

1st year: $37,428 (GS-9)

THE SCOOP

Financial security for all

In 1934 President Franklin Roosevelt convened a special committee on economic insecurity, comprised of the heads of the departments of Labor, Agriculture and the Treasury as well as the Attorney General and the Federal Emergency Relief Administrator. After a year of research, they presented Roosevelt with their recommendations, which became the basis for the passage of the Social Security Act in August 1935. The program was originally set up solely to provide retirement benefits to workers 65 years or older – and, for the first few years, in lump-sum payments – but amendments to the Act in 1939 provided additional benefits for spouses and minors and for the surviving families of prematurely deceased workers, while the 1950s saw the first major expansion of disability benefits and the introduction of cost-of-living increases. The Social Security Administration (SSA) also manages Supplemental Security Income (SSI) for elderly or disabled people with low incomes.

No fair cheating

The SSA established an inspector general's office in 1995 to streamline the process of auditing the agency's programs and investigating allegations of fraud. The office's investigation branch played a crucial role in building a case against Paul Mateyka, 61, of Minnesota, who began receiving disability benefits in 1988, citing back and neck injuries. But while he was receiving his monthly checks, he also co-owned and managed a laundry and tanning salon. After investigators videotaped him lifting heavy objects at the work site, he pled guilty to Social Security fraud and wire fraud and was sentenced in September 2002 to a year in prison and restitution of more than $200,000 in benefits.

Earlier in the year, Edward Birtic, a 75-year-old resident of Finksburg, Md., pled guilty to defrauding Social Security of $47,000 by failing to report his mother's death in 1994. Because the benefit checks were directly deposited into a joint account, nobody at the agency noticed that the mother was no longer alive. It wasn't until the Justice Department's Environmental Crimes Unit began an unrelated investigation of Birtic that his ruse was discovered. His one-year sentence was suspended and he was placed on supervised probation.

You get none, nuns

For years, 21 elderly nuns at the Marian Hall Home in Bellevue, Penn., had been denied full SSI benefits because the Social Security office had decided that the support they received from the Catholic Church counted as income. Administrative law judges had ruled twice in the sisters' favor but were overruled by the administration, so the nuns hired lawyers to press the appeals board handling their case to issue a formal ruling. A call from their U.S. representative to the Social Security Commissioner in March 2002 got the problem solved within hours, and the nuns were awarded full benefits, although their attorneys still anticipated some wrangling over seven year's worth of back payments.

21st century twists

The SSA has found itself trying to sort out several claims for survivor benefits involving children conceived through in vitro fertilization using the sperm of deceased males, a task further complicated by the differences in inheritance law from one state to the next. After an administrative law judge determined that two Arizona children did not qualify as legitimate offspring or dependents of the sperm donor, his widow filed a federal lawsuit charging a constitutional rights violation. Her case was buttressed by a January 2002 ruling by the Massachusetts Supreme Judicial Court that acknowledged posthumously conceived children as legal heirs, in cases where parentage and consent to posthumous conception can both be proven. A similar case in Renton, Wash., was further complicated by the fact that the mother had not married her fiancé before he died of brain cancer in 1994.

GETTING HIRED

The Social Security Administration hires entry-level lawyers as staff attorneys, and lawyers with seven years of experience as administrative law judges. The SSA hires at regional offices all around the country. Check the agency's web site, www.ssa.gov, for contact information.

The SSA hires at regional offices all around the country.

Trial Lawyers for Public Justice

1717 Massachusetts Avenue NW
Suite 800
Washington, DC 20036
Phone: (202) 797-8600
www.tlpj.org

LOCATIONS

Washington, DC (HQ)
Oakland, CA

THE STATS

No. of attorneys: 11
No. of other employees: 16
Executive Director: Arthur H.
Bryant

THE SCOOP

Fighting for public justice

Founded in 1982, Trial Lawyers for Public Justic (TLPJ) is the only national public interest law firm that marshals the skills and resources of trial lawyers for the public good. TLPJ brings socially significant impact litigation to protect consumers, preserve the environment, stand up for civil rights, hold governmental and corporate wrongdoers accountable, and safeguard access to the civil justice system. TLPJ is the principal project of the TLPJ Foundation, which draws upon the support of over 2,700 members nationwide.

TLPJ is noted for the wide range of legal issues to which it devotes its resources. It has filed more Title IX gender discrimination cases than any other law firm, and has successfully resolved every one, including their landmark Supreme Court victory in Cohen v. Brown University. TLPJ's Class Action Abuse Prevention Project files objections to proposed settlements that would net hefty fees for attorneys and let corporate offenders off the hook without implementing reforms or seeking compensation for class members. A Mandatory Arbitration Abuse Prevention Project seeks to preserve the right of injured or deceived consumers to have their day in court. Project Access fights unnecessary court secrecy, including secret settlements that would keep the public in the dark about dangerously defective tires and other products. And the Environmental Enforcement Project brings citizen enforcement suits to protect our nation's clean air and clean water, including the fight against mountaintop removal mining in West Virginia.

Consumer rights

The TLPJ appeared in the Supreme Court's chambers in October 2002 to argue on behalf of consumers who suffered disabling or fatal injuries in boating accidents involving boat engines without propeller guards. The husband of Jeanne Sprietsma had filed a wrongful death suit brought against Mercury Marine, the manufacturers of the outboard engine whose propeller struck and killed her after she fell out of a recreational boat. But the trial court granted Mercury Marine's motion to dismiss on the grounds that federal boating safety laws and Coast Guard policy preempted the ability of victims in such accidents to seek legal redress under state law. TLPJ's argument to reverse this ruling, supported by the Solicitor General's office and the attorneys general of 17 states, was unanimously approved by the justices in early December.

WTO aftershocks

During the 1999 World Trade Organization conference in Seattle, approximately 140 people were arrested both inside and outside a 24-square-block "no-protest zone" established by the city's leaders. TLPJ's class-action lawsuit against the city for violating the protestors' rights to free speech and assembly was originally filed in 2000, and received certification from a federal judge in November 2002. Although Seattle officials claimed that the individual circumstances of each arrest might invalidate class treatment, the court ruled that since the plaintiffs "were arrested together at the same general location, for the same alleged violation, and they were booked on the same charge," class-action status was appropriate.

GETTING HIRED

TLPJ's website, www.tlpj.org, posts announcements of job openings and available fellowships. The site's online database also contains links to 2,300 public interest organizations in all 50 states plus online resources for law students seeking jobs. For staff attorney positions, litigation experience is valuable, but the firm also seeks research and analytic skills. The Baron-Brayton Fellowship and Goldberg-Dietzler Fellowship are two-year programs that give recent graduates the opportunity to take an active role in developing and assisting in the litigation of TLPJ's cases and work closely with other public interest groups. Second- and third-year law students can also apply for summer internships in the firm's DC headquarters or Oakland branch office.

The Baron-Brayton Fellowship and Goldberg-Dietzler Fellowship give recent grads the opportunity to work closely with other public interest groups.

United States Air Force Judge Advocate General

HQ USAF/JAX
1420 Air Force Pentagon
Rm SB269
Washington, DC 20330-1420
www.jagusaf.hq.af.mil

LOCATIONS

Maxwell AFB, AL
85 bases worldwide

MAJOR DEPARTMENTS & PRACTICES

Administrative
Claims/Torts/Medical Malpractice
Criminal/Defense/Appellate Level
Environmental
General Litigation
Government Contracts
International and Operations Law
Labor Law
Legal Assistance

THE STATS

No. of attorneys: 1,350 active-duty officers
Judge Advocate General: Major General Thomas J. Fiscus, USAF

BASE SALARY

1st year: $34,934 (not including food and housing allowances)

EMPLOYMENT CONTACT

Chief, Recruiting Branch
1420 Air Force
Pentagon
Washington, DC 20330-1420
Phone: (800) JAG-USAF

THE SCOOP

Aim high

The Army Air Corps first acquired a judge advocate staff in 1939, and Air Judge Advocate Colonel Desmond O'Keefe retained his title when the Air Force was spun off into a separate military division eight years later. So though Congress didn't pass legislation creating an office for an Air Force Judge Advocate General until 1948, there were already more than 200 USAF Judge Advocates serving before the first JAG, Major General Reginald C. Harmon, reported for his new duties. Harmon chose to keep his staff closely connected to the rest of the Air Force, so the Air Force Judge Advocate General's Department was never designated a separate corps as was the case with JAG staff in other branches of the military. New staff members receive military legal training from instructors at the JAG School at Maxwell Air Force Base, Ala., after which they are assigned to one of the many USAF bases throughout the United States and overseas in Europe, Asia and Turkey. In addition to the basic salary, judge advocates receive a variable housing allowance, which factors in their location and family status, plus full health and dental care at any U.S. military medical facility. The training and subsequent tours of duty allow judge advocates to experience a widely diversified legal practice, encompassing not just the Uniform Code of Military Justice but everything from claims and torts to international law, as well as litigate cases very early in their legal careers.

Don't ask, don't tell, don't recruit

The Air Force Judge Advocate General's department recruits at law school campuses throughout the United States, but in many cases its presence, along with that of recruiters from the military's other JAG offices, is only grudgingly tolerated by the hosting institutions. Throughout the 1980s and 1990s, several colleges and universities adopted policies banning employers that engaged in discrimination from participating in job fairs or other interview programs; the branches of the armed forces were excluded because of their exclusionary policy towards gays and lesbians. But when the federal government threatened to withhold millions of dollars in research funding, Yale Law School elected to allow an Air Force JAG recruiter to participate in their October 2002 Fall Interview Program.

A current case

The Air Force JAG has been investigating the "friendly fire" deaths of four Canadian soldiers in Afghanistan. In April 2002, an American F-16 from the Illinois Air National Guard on a nighttime combat patrol spotted what the pilot thought was anti-aircraft fire and dropped a bomb on the site. The "hostile gunfire" was actually target practice by Canadian infantry troops on a training mission. In January 2003, an Article 32 hearing (the military equivalent of grand jury proceedings) to determine whether the F-16 pilot and his flight commander would face court-martial and manslaughter charges revealed that the pilot had dropped the bomb in a seconds-long interval between orders from air combat control officers to wait for further instructions and then to evacuate the area immediately.

GETTING HIRED

Third-year law students and practicing attorneys can earn a direct appointment as a judge advocate general. Applicants must bring a resume, complete undergraduate and law school transcripts (along with references and other supporting material) to an interview with a senior attorney at any Air Force base. The JAG officer's report and the application are forwarded to JAG headquarters where a panel of senior judge advocates consider each candidate. Grades, extracurricular activities, work experience and military service are all factored into the decision. If selected, applicants must pass a medical exam before being appointed a first lieutenant. JAG lieutenants are eligible for promotion to captain after six months; the initial commitment is four years. Ninety percent of all judge advocates are promoted to the rank of major six years after the start of their careers; slightly more than half of all appointees last the 18 years necessary to become colonels.

Second- and first-year law students can apply to the JAG Corps through the One Year College Program and the Graduate Law Program, respectively. Both programs require application to an ROTC program (which includes several weeks of field training) and an interview with a senior attorney. Law school graduates are appointed as second lieutenants and become first lieutenants upon admission to the bar and completion of necessary training programs.

Slightly more than half of all Air Force JAG appointees last the 18 years necessary to become colonels.

United States Army Judge Advocate General

Office of The Judge Advocate
  General
1777 North Kent Street, 5th Floor
Rosslyn, VA 22209-2194
Phone: (703) 588-6799
www.jagcnet.army.mil

MAJOR DEPARTMENTS & PRACTICES

Civil
Claims and Tort Litigation
Criminal
Environmental
Government Contract
International
Labor
Legal Assistance
Operational
Real Property

THE STATS

No. of attorneys: 1,500 active-duty
JAG officers
No. of other employees: 482,000
Judge Advocate General: Major
General Thomas J. Romig, U.S.
Army

BASE SALARY

1st year: $27,612

EMPLOYMENT CONTACT

www.jagcnet.army.mil/Recruiting

THE SCOOP

You're in the courtroom now

Judge advocates have served in the American military since before the formation of the United States government. The first Judge Advocate of the Army was appointed in 1775 by the Second Continental Congress, and over a dozen judge advocates served during the Revolutionary War, including future Supreme Court Chief Justice John Marshall. (Years later, future founder of the American Civil Liberties Union and Supreme Court Justice Felix Frankfurter would serve as a judge advocate during the First World War.) Although Congress abolished the position in 1802, it was reinstated 47 years later and provided with a staff of thirty-three officers shortly after the beginning of the Civil War. Today the Corps has expanded to include nearly 1,500 active-duty officers who receive military legal training at a JAG School at the University of Virginia Law School campus.

JAG staff have been deployed with front-line combat units since the 1983 invasion of Grenada, and play a critical role in the ongoing war against terrorism, at tactical positions in Afghanistan and elsewhere and in the corridors of the Pentagon. They advise troops on the legality of raids or missile strikes, evaluating whether the proposed targets are actual military sites and considering the risk of civilian deaths. JAG staff cannot authorize or call off a military assault, but they provide valuable legal advice to the commanders who do make the final decisions.

GETTING HIRED

Prospective Army lawyers must submit an application that includes an official JAG application (available at www.jagcnet.army.mil), a resume, undergraduate, graduate (where applicable) and law school transcripts and proof of bar membership to the JAG recruiting office in Rosslyn, Va. After a screening interview, applications are reviewed by a board of JAG officers. Those that make the cut are appointed to three-year commissions. Reserve officers undergo a similar screening process. The Army hires summer interns for the JAG Corps. All summer positions are civilian posts and interns are not obligated to do further military service.

United States Navy Judge Advocate General

1322 Patterson Avenue, SE
Suite 3000
Washington Navy Yard, DC 20374
http://www.jag.navy.mil

LOCATIONS

Washington, DC (HQ)
Arlington, VA

MAJOR DEPARTMENTS & PRACTICES

Civil
Claims and Tort Litigation
Criminal
Environmental
Government Contract
International
Labor
Legal assistance
Operational
Real Property

THE STATS

No. of attorneys: 840 (active-duty JAG officers)
No. of other employees: 384,311
Judge Advocate General: Rear Admiral Michael F. Lohr, USN

BASE SALARY

1st year: $33,552

EMPLOYMENT CONTACT

www.jag.navy.mil/html/
   welcome_recruit.htm

THE SCOOP

Married to the sea

The United States Navy had no legal officers until the Civil War, as naval regulations were so straightforward that nobody saw a need for lawyers to interpret them. But as courts-martial during the war became more complicated, the Secretary of the Navy borrowed an assistant U.S. Attorney and appointed him as the Navy's solicitor. He did so on his own authority, but in 1865 Congress made the post of Solicitor and Naval Judge Advocate General an official presidential appointment, albeit on a year-to-year basis. It wasn't until 1878 that the position was granted to a uniformed military officer, Col. William Butler Remey of the United States Marine Corps. Remey convinced Congress the post should always be held by a naval or marine officer chosen from within the ranks.

In 1950 Congress passed legislation creating the Uniform Code of Military Justice, and also required for the first time that the JAGs of any military branch be a lawyer with at least eight years of military service, although the Navy also had "law specialists" who did not necessarily belong to the bar but could perform legal services. Seventeen years later, however, the Judge Advocate General's Corps created a professional role for lawyers within the Navy. Today, more than 730 judge advocates litigate cases that touch upon nearly every aspect of the law at naval facilities worldwide. Staff members are provided with special legal training at the Naval Justice School, based in Newport, R. I.

GETTING HIRED

Law school students may apply to the JAG Corps Student Program after their first year. Applications are screened by location regional boards; each board is limited to a 50 percent maximum acceptance rate. Upon acceptance, JAG recruits do six weeks in Officer Indoctrination School, then nine weeks at Naval Justice School, both in Newport, R.I. A two-week indoctrination period on a naval vessel follows, then a four-year commitment. A very small number (approximately five per year) of experienced attorneys are appointed Navy JAG officers. The Navy specifically seeks experienced trial litigators for those positions.

Vera Institute of Justice

233 Broadway, 12th Floor
New York, NY 10279
Phone: (212) 334-1300
www.vera.org

LOCATIONS

New York, NY (HQ)

THE STATS

No. of attorneys: 19
No. of other employees: 130
Director: Christopher E. Stone
General Counsel: Karen Goldstein

THE SCOOP

Criminal justice reform, one step at a time

Louis Schweitzer and Herb Sturz launched the Vera Foundation in 1961 to address economic disparity in New York City's criminal court system. The two crusaders worked with the city's criminal justice leaders to create a means by which defendants with limited financial resources could be released pending trial if they could demonstrate strong community ties. Their idea proved effective, and has influenced the way arraignments are processed in courts throughout the United States and abroad. A 1966 grant from the Ford Foundation allowed Schweitzer and Sturz to expand their organization, which they renamed the Vera Institute of Justice.

The Institute has substantially broadened its operations since then, applying its efforts to nearly every facet of the criminal justice system. It has provided a helping hand to the judicial branch of the South African government as it struggles to cope with a broad new set of responsibilities, and has led a series of international conferences on policing in democratic societies. It has analyzed drug treatment programs that serve as alternatives to incarceration for many criminal offenders, and helped create a test program in New York City that works with soon-to-be-released prisoners to prepare them for freedom and help them avoid returning to a life of crime. In order to maintain this diverse range of innovative programs, Vera continually spins off its programs into government agencies or other nonprofit organizations. In most cases, Vera lays the groundwork for a new nonprofit that can continue to serve the community independently. Successful nonprofits that got their start at the Vera Institute include the Neighborhood Defender Service of Harlem, the victim assistance organization Safe Horizon and the Center for Employment Opportunities, which provides job training for ex-offenders.

GETTING HIRED

You'll find a full listing of available positions at the Vera Institute's web site, www.vera.org. It includes several internships that will give you an immediate introduction to the nitty-gritty of criminal justice reform. Although Vera has a small counsel's office, other lawyers work in the Institute's program areas and are not practicing law.

Psst...
Need a Change in Venue?

Use the Internet's most targeted

job search tools for law

professionals.

Vault Law Job Board

The most comprehensive and convenient job board for law professionals. Target your search by area of law, function, and experience level, and find the job openings that you want. No surfing required.

VaultMatch Resume Database

Vault takes match-making to the next level: post your resume and customize your search by area of law, experience and more. We'll match job listings with your interests and criteria and e-mail them directly to your inbox.

APPENDIX

Alphabetical List of Legal Employers

American Civil Liberties Union 12

Central Intelligence Agency (CIA) 16

Cook County State's Attorney's Office 20

DC Employment Justice Center 24

Department of Agriculture 26

Department of Commerce 30

Department of Education 34

Department of Energy 38

Department of Health and Human Services 42

Department of Housing and Urban Development (HUD) 46

Department of the Interior 50

Department of Justice (DOJ) 54

Department of Labor 60

Department of State 64

Department of the Treasury 68

Drug Enforcement Administration (DEA) 72

Environmental Protection Agency (EPA) 76

Federal Aviation Administration (FAA) 80

Federal Bureau of Investigation (FBI) 84

Federal Communications Commission (FCC) .88

Federal Election Commission (FEC) 94

Federal Emergency Management Agency (FEMA) 98

Federal Reserve Board 102

Federal Trade Commission (FTC) 106

General Accounting Office (GAO) 110

General Services Administration 114

Human Rights Watch 118

Internal Revenue Service (IRS) 124

Lawyers Committee for Human Rights 128

Lawyers' Committee for Civil Rights Under Law 132

Legal Aid Society of New York 136

Los Angeles County District Attorney 140

Mexican American Legal Defense and Educational Fund (MALDEF) . .144

Manhattan District Attorney 148
National Association for the Advancement of Colored People (NAACP) .152
National Asian Pacific American Legal Consortium 156
National Association of State PIRGs 160
National Women's Law Center 164
Nuclear Regulatory Commission 168
Occupational Safety and Health Administration (OSHA) 172
Office of the Comptroller of the Currency 176
Patent and Trademark Office 180
Security and Exchange Commission (SEC) 184
Social Security Administration 188
Trial Lawyers for Public Justice 192
United States Air Force Judge Advocate General 196
United States Army Judge Advocate General .200
United States Navy Judge Advocate General .202
Vera Institute of Justice 204

About the Author

Ron Hogan

Ron Hogan is a freelance writer currently based in New York. He also publishes the popular literary web site Beatrice.com.

Psst...
Need a Change in Venue?

Use the Internet's most targeted

job search tools for law

professionals.

Vault Law Job Board

The most comprehensive and convenient job board for law professionals. Target your search by area of law, function, and experience level, and find the job openings that you want. No surfing required.

VaultMatch Resume Database

Vault takes match-making to the next level: post your resume and customize your search by area of law, experience and more. We'll match job listings with your interests and criteria and e-mail them directly to your inbox.

VAULT
> the most trusted name in career information™